1968

W9-AOX-346

This book may be kept

FOURTEEN DAYS

A fine will be charged for each day the book is kept overtime.

GAYLORD 142			PRINTED IN U.S.A.

YALE ROMANIC STUDIES, SECOND SERIES, 15

PATTERNS OF FAILURE IN

La Comédie humaine

by Charles Affron

New Haven and London, Yale University Press, 1966

FOR MIRELLA

"Benedette le voci"

Acknowledgments

I am delighted to thank now, in some small way, the people without whose encouragement and advice this book would not have been written: Jean Boorsch, in whose graduate course I did my first research on Balzac; Henri Peyre who has followed the progress of an idea through its birth in a doctoral thesis to its fruition in book form, and whose aid and inspiration were always forthcoming; Victor Brombert for his timely and acute suggestions; and Kenneth Cornell whose unflagging patience and generous criticism helped nurture the manuscript in its final stages.

I also wish to express my gratitude to the French government for the grant that made much of my research possible, and to Brandeis University for providing funds for the typing of the manuscript.

C. A.

New York City
February 1966

Contents

Introduction

Failure is an end to which men and events gravitate, downward to dissolution and oblivion. With brutal finality, it serves up a judgment for all that has preceded. Actually, it is a summation, where each element of an existence is seen in retrospect and finely weighed for evaluation.

An analysis of failure in *La Comédie humaine* must begin by placing this theme within the philosophical framework that Balzac bestows upon his novels, for only then can the extent of its significance be perceived. In outlining the relationship between failure and the laws that function in the author's fictional universe one comes to realize that these two elements are mutually revealing. If failure takes on relief when seen in conjunction with the system within which it operates, that system itself is in turn characterized by the implacability of failure. The theme takes relevance from the context, and the context is colored by the theme. Behind all of this stands the creator, the guiding spirit whose fatalistic cast imposes failure upon most of the characters in *La Comédie humaine*. Through the theme emerges the man who obeys the tragic compulsion to judge and doom the inhabitants of his fictional world, the man who sees all too clearly that an infraction of the rules set down by the forces governing this world leads to inevitable defeat. Failure thus offers a threefold interest: its intrinsic value as a theme, its role in the total scheme of the novels, and its importance in the author's realistic pessimism.

Balzac keeps no secrets from his readers. While he sometimes surprises with twists of irony, touches of melodrama, and even an occasional deus ex machina, he takes careful pains to render the overall direction of *La Comédie humaine* readily apparent. There are countless signposts, guides through the tortuous, densely populated, and unflaggingly detailed world which the author seeks to describe. Balzac has a pressing need to define this direction, to explain the laws that govern it, to cite other systems and theories that bolster and supposedly give it credence. The shape of *La Comédie humaine* is impressed on practically every incident, and each character takes his place in a gallery of figures that is meant to amplify and fill out this shape. There is a monolithic mechanism which looms up out of prefaces, out of the mouths of characters, and out of thinly disguised digressions within the novels themselves. The hero's physiognomy, his past, his place in society, the clothes he wears, the room he lives in, all are summoned as testimony to his behavior and to the events in which he participates. Balzac wants the reader to feel that the workings of this fictional universe and the lives of the beings who belong there are not products of a creative whimsey, but are reflections of a universal truth. There is a conscious effort to refashion the novel by making it an instrument of scientific reporting or philosophical definition. It becomes an illustration of axioms that the author postulates.[1] The zoologist formulates his theories about the animal kingdom; Balzac projects similar methods upon the area of human behavior and shares the scientist's conviction as to the truth and validity of his findings. In the preface to *La Comédie humaine* he describes the similarity between the world of nature and the organization of human society.

Does not Society make of man, according to the environments in which the events of his life unfold, as many

1. Pierre Laubriet, in *L'Intelligence de l'art chez Balzac* (Paris, 1961), studies in great detail the author's artistic self-awareness.

different men as there are varieties in zoölogy? . . . Thus, there have always existed, and there will exist for all time Social Species, as there are Zoölogical Species. Just as Buffon did a magnificent job in trying to represent in a book the totality of Zoology, was there not a work of this type to be done for Society? (Avant-propos à *La Comédie humaine, 1, 4*)[2]

Balzac proposes to take on such a task and, in doing so, hopes that his novels will have a truth and a validity uncommon to the form. As a result, the matter of *La Comédie humaine* comes into the world stretched taut by forces that are constant from novel to novel, forces that eternally operate on the "Social Species."

The author evokes an assortment of ready-made theories upon which he builds his own system.[3] Cuvier, St. Hilaire, Buffon, and Swedenborg are wont to enter the novels, stopping the action with their tirades of outdated sententiousness. These little pseudo-scientific, metaphysical, and spiritualistic digressions graphically demonstrate Balzac's desire to anchor the imaginative securely in what he considers extra-fictional truth. Nor can one dismiss the prefaces written by the novelist himself and his propagandists, Félix Davin and Philarète Chasles. Their bravado, palaver, and honest-to-goodness salesmanship notwithstanding, many of the reasons and motives they enunciate are truly reflected in the novels.

Balzac posits a fictional world where chance has its place, but where, more often, events and human beings proceed down furrows of a destiny quite easily charted by the reader in advance. There is a steadily rumbling machine that gives *La*

2. The extracts cited from Balzac's works, unless otherwise indicated, are drawn from the edition of *La Comédie humaine* published by the Bibliothèque de la Pléiade (Paris, 1935–62). Balzac wrote the "Avant-propos à *La Comédie humaine*" for the Furne edition in 1842. All translations from the French are my own.

3. See Laubriet, pp. 253–320.

Comédie humaine its consistency. Each character comes into the world armed with qualities that the author has labeled, time after time, as liabilities or advantages. An analogy with classical tragedy imposes itself here. For the Greeks, the tragic hero is doomed because he possesses some trait that makes him incongruent with the order of things, created by the gods and belonging to a body of knowledge, a repertoire of myth and religion familiar to the public. The inevitability of the hero's fate is one of his strongest links to the audience, and the macabre fascination that rivets one's attention to the condemned man is a taste Balzac too eagerly tries to satisfy. By first garbing his novels in prefaces and asides which are the bylaws of his fictional world, and then introducing characters with comments that immediately reveal their flaws, he transports the reader to a sphere for which he has made all the rules. Like the omnipotent gods, he stands over his creation, forcing each of his subjects to be seen in perspective against a finely wrought background. The credence that grips one in the face of Greek tragedy is similar to the reader's conviction that the Balzacian heroes are truthfully portrayed in relation to the frame in which they are placed. As each man's fate is sealed the reader nods in silent approval.

A realization of the author's assumptions and an ability to recognize the forces constantly present as he introduces characters and generates plots make one sensitive to the deterministic unfolding of the fabulation. A thematic study must take into consideration the rigidly constructed world that the author has made, for in dealing with this sort of determinism, each theme must be viewed as a function of the total mechanism that is in operation. A theme takes on a special aura when it finds its locus in a definite construct, when it impinges upon everything within that construct.

The presence of failure in *La Comédie humaine* indicates that some obstacle is in conflict with the steady pulsation of forces governing the system that Balzac has created. It shows how a particular element is poorly integrated into the great mechanism, and it then becomes immediately apparent that the trick of success is to fit oneself into this mechanism, into the order of the universe. The failure of the Balzacian character depends upon an imperfect interpretation of the forces that control his life, on an unwillingness to make the compromises necessary for conforming to them, or on an inability to fashion his life according to them. In a sense, each novel is the account of this relationship between the human element, governed by the intelligence, and the unyielding matter of reality, constituted by the forces that lie beyond man's control, the constants that must be reckoned with rather than defied or ignored. The choices that the intelligence makes in the struggle characterizing this relationship form the plot of the novel, and the success or failure of the choices provokes the dénouement.

Failure is a versatile focus into *La Comédie humaine.* It does not simply illuminate the machinelike forces that govern man's existence, for Balzac does not coldly eye man struggling with the world. He has opinions about the struggle, as well as about the forces at work. The way in which failure occurs, its place in the dénouement, the type of character that fails, the tone used in describing failure, all these factors contribute to the revelation of two sides of the author's nature. On the one hand, he is the grim realist who perceives the great mechanism, who is convinced of its truth, and who has willingly assumed the task of describing it. But on the other hand, he is the sentimental idealist who admires certain human contests that are waged against overwhelming forces, and the humanist who is inordinately proud that such a struggle can be waged at all. The unhappy compromise between fatalistic determinism and romantic spiritualism is shown no more vividly than by the failure of the ideals in which the author so ardently wishes to believe.

There is another aspect of *La Comédie humaine* that is involved in the theme of failure. Since a deterministic functioning of the universe lies at the base of Balzac's thought, and since it is the validity of this theory that he seeks to illustrate, determinism's role as a literary device must be investigated. Just as it is intrinsic to the understanding of the philosophical foundations of *La Comédie humaine*, it is also intrinsic to the understanding of Balzac's aesthetics. Fatalistic determinism is a literary fact, incorporated into the novels and referred to by the characters. Failure's particular resonance in Balzac is an added reminder that no event and no individual destiny is unrelated to the web that links the seemingly incongruous elements of reality. This web is one of the most unusual novelistic devices among Balzac's literary inventions.

Finally, failure serves as an appropriate pretext for discussing several major elements of Balzac's rhetoric and imagery. The theme, a basic one in the structure of *La Comédie humaine*, earns a full barrage of Balzacian literary display. It stimulates his imagination to create a variety of expression, setting off the different manifestations of the theme. This variety is misleading, however, for the frequent recurrence of devices like reflection, juxtaposition, and contrast is a constant reminder of the artistic unity that functions within *La Comédie humaine*. Failure serves to organize such devices, to place them within a workable context.

Thus, by investigating the theme of failure, the situation of the character in the world of the novelist will be made clear, the creator's values will be defined, and the connection between his personal philosophy and his literary method will be underlined. Having at once an ideological and stylistic importance, failure offers a particularly prominent vantage point from which to survey the vast and sprawling thing that is *La Comédie humaine*.

CHAPTER 1

Precedents and Laws

One might hesitate at synthesizing, without chronological consideration, an author's universe. Of course, Balzac's ideas change, and in regard to his political convictions, in a remarkably short span of years. Yet the basic statement of purpose he sets forth in the prefaces and assorted pronouncements that dot his novels' textures is not liable to radical fluctuation throughout his career. The passions and excesses that haunt the novels of 1830 are the same passions and excesses that he condemns in 1846. The order of the world and the need to find meaning in chaos are preoccupations of Balzac long before *La Comédie humaine* is fully conceived. A cogent digest of theoretical statements gives a faithful picture of his work's totality.

What a boon it would have been for us if some Roman author had had the courage to brave the critics (who, without a doubt, would have condemned him for describing Roman life to the Romans), by making studies of moeurs in the first century of the Christian era, between the reign of Caesar and that of Nero, by describing to us the thousand details, the typical and grandiose existences of that vast empire! It is also principally the job of the author to arrive at synthesis through analysis, to depict and to assemble the elements of our life, to introduce the

themes and to work them out together, finally to trace
the immense aspect of a century by painting its principal
characters. (Préface d'*Une Fille d'Eve*, 11, 376–77)

There are many such statements, but this one seems particularly appropriate since it contains, in germ, Balzac's method
and attitude toward his mission. His object is to deduce universal
truths from individual case histories based, of course, on the
assumption that universal truths exist, that there are laws and
forces that apply to all men's lives.

> In this world, every effect has a cause and every cause a
> principle, every principle is dependent upon a law. The
> principles which have created extraordinary men can be
> studied and known. Nothing is unimportant, neither the
> condition of father, nor that of mother, neither posture,
> nor season, nor former nourishment, nor places, nor
> images.[1]

Balzac states here a very firm commitment to a deterministic
philosophy. The importance of this kind of thinking in his
aesthetics of the novel is immediately evident. If men can be
studied with some precision, if in fact their lives can be minutely
dissected, one tends to believe that a meaningful correlation
of data drawn therefrom can be accomplished. In an effort to
synthesize, Balzac makes generalizations from one man's existence. He proposes to fill in his fresco of the nineteenth century
with faces chosen because they possess traits common to all
faces. He points to themes that haunt mankind by showing
their application to the life of a single man, and he places each
character in the cadre of town, city, and family, thereby describing the interaction of all men in their societal contexts. In each
novel he faithfully attempts to relate the particular to the
general. This is Balzac's basic method. Let us not forget, how-

1. Honoré de Balzac, *Pensées, sujets, fragmens*, Préface et notes de
Jacques Crépet (Paris, 1910), p. 156.

ever, his nostalgia for the perceptive Roman who never wrote the history of daily life during the first century A.D. Balzac admits that this scribe and analyst would have incurred blame, the same blame that he himself incurs in the nineteenth century. This is a sensitive point. In the preface to *Le Père Goriot*[2] Balzac makes a list of virtuous characters, showing that they outnumber the wicked ones in his novels. This list is at once an answer to his censors and a reassuring act of self-congratulation on the part of a novelist who still endeavors to defend his genre on didactic terms. But the arithmetic of the list is not convincing. The virtuous heroines are, for the most part, unhappy, defeated heroines. The evil characters and the evil plots that they engender are the true motors of *La Comédie humaine*. Balzac, in seeking to elucidate "the elements of our life," commits himself to an honest appraisal of his times. He speaks of courage on the part of the hypothetical Roman because he knows that the picture of his own contemporary reality is not a pretty one. It evokes cries of censure, because the good so often fail at the expense of the wicked. No amount of Paulines can whitewash the sins of the Foedoras and, what is more important, no amount of Paulines can vanquish the Foedoras. The sterling homilies offered by the virtuous Madame de Mortsauf to Félix de Vandenesse, are overwhelmed by the insistence and conviction of another brand of advice—the grim facts of life as told by de Marsay and Vautrin. The references to the amalgamation of a thousand details, the analysis and the synthesis—these terms borrowed from a scientific-philosophic vocabulary—betray the author's search for evidence of any kind, his passion for seeing all the threads, both pretty and ugly, that make up the surface design. His need to excuse himself because the ugly ones are more

2. Composed for the first edition, though entitled "Préface de la 2ème édition" (Balzac considered as the first edition of the novel its publication in *La Revue de Paris*), this preface was omitted after 1839. It can be found in the Pléiade edition, vol. 11.

numerous than the pretty does not prevent him from reaching a sobering conclusion: at least insofar as the world measures success, the good succeed less often than the wicked.

The thousand details of *La Comédie humaine* do not rob any significance from the single detail. The failure of a particular character transcends his special condition, has some meaning beyond the moment and the individual. It fits into the grandiose scheme of the author, where no detail is gratuitous, and the destiny of no man meaningless. By studying one failure, by detailing its moment in time, its causes and its outcome, Balzac hopes to achieve a universal definition of failure.[3] The confusions of life are reconcilable. Failure is simply one of the ordering references employed by the author.

In this process of generalization of individual and incident, Balzac's next step is a logical one.

> In order to merit the praises which any artist must covet, did I not have to study the reasons or the reason for these social effects, to ferret out the sense hidden in this immense assemblage of faces, of passions and of events? Finally, after having searched for, I do not say found, this reason, this social motor, was it not necessary to meditate upon the natural principles and to see how Societies stray from or approach the eternal rule of truth, of beauty? (Avant-propos à *La Comédie humaine, 1, 7*)

A belief in the standardization of certain human qualities and in the pertinence of typical human situations betrays a belief in the existence of the "social motor." Balzac also suggests that there is a divergence between this machine and the eternal rules of truth and beauty, a divergence which will be discussed later. Here one must simply recognize the extent of Balzac's allegiance to a deterministic view of the universe. Effects, hidden

3. Maurice Bardèche, in *Balzac romancier* (Paris, 1940), pp. 372–77, is particularly eloquent in his appraisal of the links between the individual and the species.

sense, and reasons are his bywords. He preaches determinism in his prefaces and shows it in action as he spins out the tale of *La Comédie humaine*. He uses it to impart truth to his fiction, giving each character's destiny an irrevocability, a rightness in the huge scheme of the world that he seeks to illustrate.[4]

Beside the generalizations and the scientific theories already mentioned there is another phenomenon—history—which points to the existence of a mechanism governing events. The spirit of revolution, the eternal dissatisfaction of populations, envy, the sameness of life through time, the constancy of these traits in the mechanism's personality are attested to by the past.

> When religion and royalty are overthrown, the people will turn on great men, after great men they will attack the rich. Finally, when Europe is only an inconsistent flock of men because it is without leaders, it will be devoured by crass conquerors. The world has already staged this spectacle twenty times, and Europe begins it anew. (*Sur Catherine de Médicis*, 10, 276–77)

The machine has always existed and will continue to exist. Obviously, the author's eye most readily seizes upon the destructive qualities of the machine, as he seeks to explain events by its presence and by its past performance. Just as the quality of man is a constant, so the quality of the forces that mold him through time remains unchanged and unchanging.

One of the strongest forces at work in *La Comédie humaine* is the law of grandeur and decadence. It accounts for relentlessly changing fashions and the elusiveness of success.

> Each existence has its peak, a moment during which the causes function and are in exact relationship to the results.

4. Ramon Fernandez, in *Balzac* (Paris, 1943), offers an important analysis of the consistency between Balzac's fiction and his social, philosophical, and political notions.

This noontime of life, when the living forces are in equilibrium and are produced in all their brilliance, is common
not only to organic beings, but also to cities, to nations,
to ideas, to institutions, to commerces, to enterprises which,
similar to noble races and to dynasties, are born, rise and
fall. From this is derived the rigor with which the theme
of growth and decay is applied to all that is organized
here on Earth, for death itself has, in time of plague, its
progress, its slackening, its recrudescence and its sleep.
Our globe itself is perhaps a flare only slightly more
durable than the others. (*César Birotteau, 5,* 366)

The effort of authentication is always at work in Balzac. Precedence is cited as proof of law. The theory of species à la
Buffon explains the organization of mankind. The fact of death,
significant in its finality, is used here as a proof of the law of
growth and decline. Human beings, ideas, and dynasties are
linked to the rhythm of death, and that rhythm is vaguely
attached to an eventual cosmic death. Balzac never declines an
opportunity to give great importance to "each existence," and
incidentally inject into his discussion passing references to
destruction.

This theory of grandeur and decadence has far-reaching
implications in the functioning of the universal organism,
implications that are only sketched in the foregoing definition.
It lies at the root of the voraciousness characteristic of the
nineteenth century, its constant demands for novelty in philosophy, in government, in beauty. Such demands spell the failure
of anyone convinced that absolutes exist in these domains. As
the law of change envelops all, the absolute standard quickly
becomes the quaint fashion and finally the superannuated con-
vention. The dying city, the dying nation, the dying commerce,
the dying school of literature condemn by contagion the blind
stalwarts clinging to their corpses. Men fail because they refuse
or are unable to take into consideration this basic law, this nat-

ural rhythm of flowering and decay, this overwhelming quality that prevails in the system to which they belong. Because they are human they have no choice. They are parts in the motor. The merciless sentence of death pronounced by the law of grandeur and decadence makes useless their principles and their absolutes. They would be wiser to listen to the advice of the sagest character in *La Comédie humaine,* Vautrin. "There are no principles, there are only events; there are no laws, there are only circumstances: the superior man espouses events and circumstances in order to control them" (*Le Père Goriot,* 2, 940). The laws and principles to which Vautrin refers are man-made rather than natural. While he chooses to scoff at codified law he is perfectly attuned to the great forces that mold time. It is this awareness that enables him to cope so successfully with events, mastering the moment and overcoming the obstacles that puny men and their laws put in his way. Vautrin will not be caught espousing the cause of a dying nation, and he knows perfectly well that the laws of the living nation have nothing permanent about them. They too will pass into disuse, but, for the present, they must be dealt with and manipulated. In the course of constantly changing events and circumstances, a course governed by this law of grandeur and decadence, one can be sure only of the inevitability of change. Voluntary submission to this law and shrewd calculations based upon it are necessary to insure success. Defiance of the inexorable flux, in the form of clinging to useless principles, leads to inevitable failure.

The second great law that controls men and events shares this fatalistic quality with the law of grandeur and decadence. It bluntly condemns ideals and those who believe in them. The classic formula, "survival of the fittest," neatly describes the play of self-interest and ambition that lies at the root of men's actions. By "fittest" Balzac means the strongest, the healthiest, the cleverest, the most ruthless men. Saintly qualities are worthless arms in the battle for survival. There are many ways of

describing *La Comédie humaine* and one of the most apt is
as a brutal, detailed report of this battle. The author points
to Paris as the arena in which the duel between men is staged,
but really, the same laws, the same grim truths apply to provincial life. This is how Félix Davin sees Balzac's Paris:

> Here, sentiments are the exceptions and are broken by
> the play of interest, crushed between the wheels of a
> mechanical world; virtue is slandered, innocence is sold,
> passions give way to ruinous tastes, to vices; everything is
> rarified, is analyzed, is bought and sold; it is a bazaar
> where all is classified; scheming is practiced openly and
> without shame, humanity has only two forms, the cheat
> and the cheated. (Introduction aux "Études de moeurs,"
> *II, 225*)[5]

With great bitterness and a moralistic, albeit realistic, tone,
Balzac shows the incompatibility of sentiments with a mechan-
ical world. In this arena where each man seeks to conquer,
where the conqueror distinguishes himself by acquiring signs
of material success, where one has only the choice between
conquering or being conquered, sentiments are useless. They
do not pay; you cannot buy anything with them.

Brute strength and cunning are the only possible safeguards.
With the former, one may resist for a while the killing pace
of the machine, and with the latter, one may perceive the
propitious moment when, from the combinations of events
and circumstances, the greatest gain may be drawn. The weak
of mind and spirit are doomed to perish because the machine,
which demands parts that fit, that insure a proper and smooth
functioning, rejects them.

> The world abhors sorrows and misfortunes, it fears them
> as it does contagions, it never hesitates between them and

5. The "Introduction aux Études de moeurs au XIXe siècle" was written
by Davin, under the close guidance of Balzac, for the Béchet edition and
appeared at the beginning of the first volume, published in 1835.

vices: vice is a luxury. No matter how majestic the misfortune, society succeeds in belittling and ridiculing it
with an epigram . . . it never pardons the gladiator who
falls; it lives on gold and mockery; "Death to the weak,"
is the vow of the competitive order instituted in all the
nations of the Earth. (*La Peau de chagrin*, 9, 220–21)

This is the cruelest article in the code of law, for it dooms not
only the good but also the weak and the ill. They are of no
utility to the machine; they have no force with which to
struggle against other men. Like weak and beautiful sentiments,
they have no buying power on the going market.

Gold, the symbol of this buying power, is the standard
against which failure or success is measured. The glib tone of
an article like "Le Code des gens honnêtes" does not dull the
violence of Balzac's attack on a world whose every value is
based on money. The struggle for survival is translated by the
nineteenth century into the amassing of gold, and no amount
of security measures taken by those who have this precious
metal will discourage the avidity of those who are without it.

Life can be considered a perpetual combat between the
rich and the poor. The former are entrenched in a fortress
with bronze walls, filled with munitions; the latter sur-
round, jump, attack, nibble at the walls and, notwithstanding the spiked machines that are erected, the doors,
the moats, the artillery, it is rare that the besiegers, these
cossacks of the social order, do not gain some advantage.[6]

6. Balzac, "Le Code des gens honnêtes," *Oeuvres complètes,* édition
Bouteron et Longnon (Paris, 1935), *38, 64.* The first edition of "Le Code
des gens honnêtes" was published anonymously in 1825. The third edition,
published in 1829 under the title "Code pénal," bears the name of Horace
Raisson, a probable collaborator of Balzac. Only in 1854, republished with
its original title, does Balzac's name appear on the title page.

Gold buys the one thing that the soulless conqueror can appreciate—pleasure, a pernicious fruit according to Balzac's standard of values. Several qualities render it reprehensible. By fostering the need for gold, it fosters the struggle between men, plunging them deeper and deeper into materialism, dooming more and more of them to failure. As more men struggle, more men fail. And perhaps what is more important, pleasure squanders productive energy, numbing and preventing a man from progressing, from improving his lot, and finally killing him. "In order to obey this universal master, pleasure or gold, one must devour time, squeeze time, find more than twenty-four hours in the day and night, become weak, kill oneself, sell thirty years of old age for two years of a sickly rest" (*La Fille aux yeux d'or*, 5, 256). Pleasure feeds on gold and this successful partnership pressures doomed men into wasting their lives on a senseless struggle, in which the only thing that they succeed in gaining is that which dooms them.

It is obvious that the several basic laws that haunt Balzac have failure built-in. As these destructive, chaotic, and uncivilized forces relentlessly function, more and more men fail. The law of grandeur and decadence decrees that all shall decay and die; it creates the god of fashion, a god who demands a constant supply of human sacrifice. And are there any victors in the struggle for survival? The victor of today is fated to be overcome by a stronger man who rises up to face him tomorrow. Balzac is aware of the disparity that exists between the human condition which forces upon men this struggle for success and the pragmatic reality of universal mechanics which quickly disposes of such success. The frequency of failure in *La Comédie humaine* is only one of the many proofs that point to man's precarious position in the mechanistic world.

Balzac offers man a tool for struggling with his fate. He turns to one of his cherished basic forces, one he uses to differentiate the human species from the animal—intelligence. It is with this intelligence that one is capable of struggling against the laws that doom him to defeat. It is the civilizing element which helps control natural avidity for pleasure and gold, which tries to create bastions of comforting tradition and order and ideals of beauty and truth that can withstand the inevitable decadence. Such agents of civilization are needed to protect the weak, the ill, and the good, so liable to suffer in the battle for survival.

The most immediate civilizing device upon which intelligence seizes is the formulation of a social pact, a system, whereby individuals living in proximity impose upon themselves some rules of conduct designed to regulate their baser desires. This is the kind of society perceived in novels like *Le Médecin de campagne* and *Le Curé de village*. It is a system in which, according to Henriette de Mortsauf, "the duke and peer owe more to the artisan and the poor man than the poor man and the artisan owe to the duke and peer," and in which one should follow this sterling maxim: "commit no crime against your own conscience, nor against the public conscience" (*Le Lys dans la vallée, 8,* 888). But Balzac is not convinced that these examples truly reflect the relationship of men to society. He feels, instead, that the individual intelligence which originally creates society is only too ready to destroy it. Somehow the desire to triumph in the struggle of conflicting interests is stronger than the desire to calm the struggle. Through his *porte-parole,* Félix Davin, Balzac describes the conflicts of self-interest, which are stimulated by opposing intelligences and which disrupt the social order.[7] "Here you see the stresses of the social mechanism. There the daily clash of moral or financial interests brings drama and occasionally crime into the heart of what is apparently the calmest family" (Introduction aux "Études philosophiques," *11,* 224). Goodwill and dispassionate justice are

7. Bernard Guyon, in his conclusion to *La Pensée politique et sociale de Balzac* (Paris, 1947), shows the author's uneasy compromise between a search for order and a recognition of the power of individual intelligence.

sacrificed when men are thrown together in society. The social mechanism created by men to be rigid and unyielding is constantly strained and defied by the self-interest that is the birthright of all human beings. The needs of the individual make themselves known, and his unflagging efforts to satisfy them at all cost are poorly controlled by the system. "Every assembly has a tendency to create principles rather than submitting to them."[8]

This leads one to believe that the very nature of the human personality is incompatible with an ordered society. The more developed the personality becomes, the less able it is to mesh with the needs of the group. Philarète Chasles sees the personalities of Foedora and Raphaël de Valentin as examples of an advanced stage in such a development. He considers the unchecked ego, which demands separateness for self-identification, to be at the core of society's dissolution. "It is that personality which gnaws at the heart and devours the entrails of the society to which we belong. As they grow, individualities become isolated; there are no more bonds, there is no more communal life" (Introduction aux "Romans et contes philosophiques," 11, 184).[9] This condition illustrates a tragic paradox. The intelligence, by growing within the human personality, destroys the system that it creates for its own salvation—society.

Society, defeated on the one hand by individuality, is further menaced by the very make-up of its own structure, a structure dictated by the spirit of self-interest. As Balzac rails against the power of the plebe, he shows how each man's fatal desire to have the maximum amount of power in governing himself negates the efficacy of popular government. According to the author, such a governmental system does nothing but procreate competition, dishonesty, and rapacity. It institutionalizes and stimulates these reprehensible human qualities.

8. Balzac, Pensées, p. 52.
9. The "Introduction aux Romans et contes philosophiques" was written by Chasles for the Gosselin edition, published in 1831.

Today, the perceptiveness of the masses has so greatly sharpened, competition has so greatly limited profits, that any fortune rapidly made is either the result of a fortuitous invention or a legal theft. Perverted by scandalous examples, small business has, particularly in the last ten years, responded to the perfidiousness of the plans of big business by tampering with raw materials. . . . The courts have been frightened by this general dishonesty. . . . The *Charte* has proclaimed the rule of money, and success has become the highest criterion in an atheistic epoch. (*Splendeurs et misères des courtisanes*, 5, 812)

The majority of men, in seeking to rule themselves, only make more acute their natural materialism. Money becomes the true god, whose worship is decreed by the laws of the land. Balzac sees in the *Charte* a document that promotes popular suffrage and therefore caters to the unenlightened and shortsighted individual, incapable of governing himself and other men with equity. The benefits that civilization is supposed to bring to all men cannot be obtained through a law-making democratic force. Balzac has no confidence in the elective power of the people, a power diffused and perverted by separate interests and ultimately wielded by the irresponsible. "A law, the will of the people! Foolishness. One might as well give a child a switch to use on himself."[10]

Amidst this democratic chaos where money-hungry individuality destroys any attempt at order, Balzac sees the possible salvation of society through a governmental scheme of absolute rule. By its expediency and farsightedness, it can deal with the disparate yearnings of the masses and the bent toward disorder and dissolution inherent in the nature of things. Man-made laws contain large loopholes which permit great acts of fraudulence. They are tempting targets against which men pit their intelli-

10. Balzac, *Pensées*, p. 52.

gence. Arbitrary power alone is capable of eliminating those loopholes. " 'Laws are spider-webs, through which pass the big flies and where the little ones are caught.' 'What are you getting at?' said Finot to Blondet. 'At absolute government, the only one in which clever enterprises against the Law can be checked! . . . Legality is killing modern society' " (*La Maison Nucingen*, 5, 652–53). This is an admission of defeat of the common man's version of law in the realm of government. Only arbitrary rule, by checking individual interest as well as popular ignorance, can put things right.

The author's political coloring depends, to a great extent, upon circumstances, friends, and snobbery. But it is still hard to discount the influence exerted on his absolutist, aristocratic political beliefs by what he considers a realistic view of the baser instincts in men. Having found the democratic process thoroughly unreliable, Balzac tries to see in the tradition of nobility a solid and lasting citadel, capable of withstanding the fury of time and the assaults of destructive self-interest. For him, the landed aristocracy is a sign of continuity, a passing on of noble blood, noble ideas, and noble wisdom. Perhaps, for fleeting instants, he sees in the nobility qualities of natural superiority and, thus, a guarantee of its eternal power.

But the view of the grim realist that lodges within the author corrects this rosy illusion, and he is forced to abandon one of his most cherished beliefs. First, he realizes that the masses resent all that is superior. There is a natural instinct in men which forces them to try to rise, to better themselves, to break down the barriers that separate the classes, to erase the distinctions that exist between those who have power and those who have not. This tendency can be traced back to the famous battle, "the survival of the fittest." Balzac calls upon the recent course of history as testimony to this phenomenon. He sees the machine working at leveling the once finely differentiated scale of stations in life.

The author is also perfectly aware that the nobility is not

exempt from the temptations and immune to the perverting forces that govern common men. On the one hand, he cannot prevent himself from expressing blind hope in the *noblesse de sang,* searching for power in the parochiality of the nobleman's education, in the purity of the nobleman's controlled environment. Yet he knows very well that, because of the way the world is made, the nobility cannot remain apart from the masses snapping hungrily at its heels. Its position already made difficult due to the changes wrought by the events of 1789, the Reign of Terror, the rise of republicanism, and the industrial revolution, the nobility has almost willingly abdicated its heritage. It refuses to take the lead in a society without real leadership and to strengthen and solidify the great reason for its uniqueness by adapting itself, without demeaning compromise, to the demands of a new society. Instead, it thinks only of self-preservation.

> Each family ruined by the revolution, ruined by the equal distribution of holdings, thought of itself alone, and not of the great aristocratic family, assuming thus that if everyone became rich, the party would be strong. What an error! Money, too, is only a sign of power. Composed of people who conserved the high traditions of fine manners, true elegance, beautiful speech, noble modesty and pride in harmony with their existence (petty affairs when they become the center of a life to which they should be simply accessories), all these families had a certain value, which spread thin, left them with only a token of their former worth. None of these families had the courage to ask itself: Are we strong enough to wield power? (*La Duchesse de Langeais,* 5, 149)

In persisting with its selfish, single-minded purpose, the aristocracy renders itself unfit to rule. Through this lack of vision and foresight, one of the controlling factors that man has chosen for putting order into the chaotic universe fails, and its

failure dooms him to failure. He is still without a solution to
his dilemma, without an arm against the forces that menace him.

Balzac turns to abstracts of morality, to principles of good
and justice which might somehow put a stop to the endless
struggle. By creating absolutes of beauty and truth, man seeks
to impose yet another order upon the machinelike world which
crushes him with its immutable natural forces. But unfortu-
nately the guardians of this morality must be ordinary men.
The lawyers, the notaries, the judges are not free from the corruption and avarice which seem to be in the very nature of
things. Due to their pathetically human qualities, they succumb
to the same forces that corrupt other men.

There is an added disadvantage germane to the position of
these administrators of justice, which finally renders them dis-
tinctly incompetent custodians of ideals. Through constant,
everyday commerce with the precepts that they are supposed
to uphold, and as a result of the recalcitrants who subvert the
precepts, they become blind to the purity of their task and come
to see only the procedural and technical aspects of their duties.
Or worse, the law courts, where human justice is reputedly held
in sanctuary, become market places where influence and vengeance are some of the commodities that are bargained and exchanged against truth. "The usurer weighs the living, the notary weighs the dead, the lawyer weighs the conscience. Obliged
to speak ceaselessly, they all replace the idea with the word, the
sentiment with the sentence, and their soul becames a larynx.
They wear themselves out and become demoralized" (*La Fille
aux yeux d'or*, 5, 263). Corruption is contagious; either the
judge gives in to the infection or somehow no longer sees its
horror.

Balzac repeatedly emphasizes the strength of the lawless and
the immoral. He is aware that the systems of law and morality
are puny and weak weapons with which to subdue the power
of ruthless self-interest. The triumph of Vautrin is the triumph

of the outlaw who is not hampered by extraneous and debilitating considerations of honesty and justice. He plunges himself wholeheartedly into the game of life and is therefore capable of meeting it on its own terms, terms that have nothing to do with moral absolutes. Following in Vautrin's footsteps, Balzac leads the reader from the petty conniving of the Pension Vauquer to the prison milieu, where one can finally assess the raw power that exists outside of society's strictures. The strength exuded by lawlessness is the strength of self-interest in its purest form. This power is free, rampant, and all-consuming since it obeys no rules and is tethered by no conventions. In addition, those who conform to most of society's rules and manage to stay out of prison may deploy this law-breaking power in an adulterated form. They tamper with the law rather than ignore it. They coat their pockets with gain from illegal business practices, trickery, and fraud. The novels of Balzac swarm with such shysters. They are the petty gangsters whereas the avowed criminals are the great wielders of untrammeled power. Against the lawless and the shrewd, against brute force and concentrated intelligence, puny morality and sickly justice have no chance.

The typical Balzacian dénouement, in which the good suffer and the evil triumph, reveals graphically that in the struggle for survival, the strongest man always wins. Virtue has no place in such a system. It cannot buy pleasure or convert influence into power or soften the blows that the honest man receives from his unscrupulous adversary.

> Strange civilization! Society awards Virtue an income of one hundred louis for its old age, a second-floor room, plenty of bread, some new scarfs, and an old woman with her children. As for Vice, if it has some courage, if it can cleverly twist an article of the Code like Turenne twisted Montecuculli,[11] Society legitimizes its stolen millions,

11. The Austrian general, Montecuculli, was outmaneuvered by the French general, Turenne, in the campaign of 1673 on the Neckar and the Rhine.

bestows decorations on it, stuffs it with honors, and weighs it down with favors. Government is, moreover, in harmony with this profoundly illogical Society. (*Melmoth réconcilié, 9*, 268)

Balzac is acutely aware of the profound inequity that exists in the justice decreed by governments, of the fact that this justice, as a faithful reflection of man's true nature, will forever favor the strong over the good. As a result, those who base their lives upon principles of good and who conduct their relations with other men according to abstracts of morality, such as honesty, generosity, and trust, are doomed to failure. There is only one truth in the world, the truth of the event. At the end of each novel the balance of failure and success rears its ugly head, and if the author decides to crown a victor it will be the clever man who uses vice to his own betterment. It will be the man who understands the importance of the event, the fact, all that is tangible in reality.

Yet Balzac admits that there is a force of justice at work in the world, even though this force is not made manifest in the usual commerce of events or in the setup of the legal system. It is divine law, the power of heaven, and how it makes its presence known on earth, its relationship to the machine that puffs heavily under the pressures of "grandeur and decadence," "survival of the fittest," and unscrupulous self-interest, is difficult to ascertain.

According to the author, divine order is a fact, and its agent on earth is the Catholic Church. In the Holy Church he hopes to see the principles of mercy and justice symbolized for the masses, who demand a vivid symbol and a deep lesson. The Church, which does not assume that they are born of their own accord, has the task of inculcating these principles into human conduct. Judged superficially, the Church seems to be an ideal vehicle for arriving at such an end. It satisfies Balzac's aristocratic tendencies, his need for rigorous system; the nature and structure of the Catholic Church presuppose a mass of population that needs guidance by superior minds. This is Balzac's deep conviction. The Catholic Church appears to him to be the ordering factor so sorely needed in a world which seems to prefer anarchy. The Church is the only civilizing influence which retains a measure of the author's confidence throughout his career. In the preface to La Comédie humaine he states that, "Thought, the principle behind evil and good, can be prepared, subdued, and directed only by religion" (Avant-propos à La Comédie humaine, 1, 8). Thought, which is at the root of independence of spirit and self-interest, must be kept in check by a strong church which will guide men's minds in the right direction.

But the Catholic Church is not completely exempt from the corruptions and the earthly temptations that torture men and force them into prostituting the remnants of their morality. Balzac's diatribe against the Church, in Jésus-Christ en Flandre,[12] reflects a mood of the moment and suffers from a smugly apocalyptic tone compounded by patent virtuosity, but nonetheless it reveals the extent to which the author willingly admits the fallibility of his ideals.

> Unfortunate woman, why have you prostituted yourself to men? In the age of passions, having become rich, you have forgotten your pure and sweet youth, your sublime devotions, your innocent ways, your fertile beliefs, and

12. The development of Jésus-Christ en Flandre is one of the most interesting and complex in La Comédie humaine. The passage under consideration here is found in its primitive form in "Zéro," a short story which appeared in La Silhouette on October 3, 1830. Balzac joined this to another story, "La Danse des pierres," and the new version, entitled L'Église, was included in the 1831 edition of Romans et contes philosophiques. In 1846 L'Église was added to Jésus-Christ en Flandre in Études philosophiques. Throughout these alterations there is no essential change in the author's pronouncement against the Church.

you have abdicated your original power, your purely intellectual supremacy over the powers of the flesh. Having
shed your linen garments, your bed of moss, your grottos
illuminated by divine lights, you have glittered with dia-
monds, with luxury and with lewdness. (*Jésus-Christ en
Flandre*, 9, 264)

The Church is seen as the poor man who comes to Paris, finds
himself surrounded by vice and a society that values only money,
and, through weakness and contagion, succumbs to the damning
temptations. Balzac is romantically nostalgic for those primitive
linen garments that symbolize a Church untainted by material
considerations. The saving of souls was done then by good works
and prayer. Conversely, the secularization of the Church's interests has contaminated the special freedom and power it once
had, a priority guaranteed by lack of concern for earthly values.
Just as the nobility sold its power by adopting the self-interest
and lack of foresight of the bourgeoisie, so the Church is power-
less if it refuses to sequester itself, to insulate itself against
unhealthy influences that come from outside its spiritual do-
main. As a result, the Catholic Church is a sometimes imperfect
tool in mankind's feeble attempt to tinker with the machine that
rules its destiny. And in rare moments of objectivity, Balzac
questions even the purity with which he usually qualifies Christian dogma. "There is no religion which does not resemble all
the others and does not produce the same effects, the same sum
of evil and the same sum of good, and this is true of governments and lesser organizations as well."[13]

Individual religiosity and piety are no less immune from
Balzac's sense of reality, from his searing and merciless glance.
"The Catholic faith is a lie which we make to ourselves. Hope
is faith in the future. Pride is faith in oneself. Piety is the ruse
of a child who behaves well in order to have some jam (or
perhaps the ruse of a miser who refuses himself everything, for

13. Balzac, *Pensées*, p. 31.

deprivation is his enjoyment)."[14] Such an ironic treatment of religion is not typical of Balzac. By the same token, one cannot deny that the author is capable of this brand of cynicism, a cynicism that has its place in the texture of *La Comédie humaine*. The failure of ideals keeps recurring lest the reader forget that nonmaterial considerations have little or no value in a materialistic world.

Society cannot govern itself, and the governing systems it concocts can have only, at best, very limited success. Balzac sees one last hope for mankind. Perhaps the great man, the genius, the artist can free himself from the influence of perfidious self-interest, insure his soul against avidity, and exercise the comprehensive view that will enable him to educate and lead the masses to a better life. This faith in the great man is one that the reader may well expect to discover in Balzac. As an author he is automatically imbued with respect for the creative artist, as an amateur philosopher he naturally believes in the power of the thinker, and the part of Balzac that has no use for democracy is certainly prejudiced in favor of the great man who belongs to an intellectual élite.

> From the spectacle of this society ceaselessly tormented in its foundations as in its effects, in its causes as in its action, in which philanthropy is a magnificent error, and progress an absurdity, I have had confirmation of the truth that life is within us and not without; that to rise above men in order to command them is the magnified role of a school monitor; and that men strong enough to climb to the point from which they can enjoy a view on worlds must not look at their feet. (*Louis Lambert*, 10, 414)

In the words of Louis Lambert, the most representative thinker in Balzac's novels, the great man must dislodge himself from

14. Ibid., pp. 30–31.

the restricting horizons of the everyday and place himself on a superior vantage point from which he will be able to see beyond and to judge the human situation in its manifold aspects. Only then can he be of any use to the world. This great man is a personification of the civilizing force of intelligence that is latent in all men, that has conceived the previously discussed systems that failed. But in the great man, intelligence is concentrated and, harking back to one of Balzac's pet theories, only through *volonté,* which is a concentration of *force vitale,* can the real strength needed in this losing struggle against the natural forces of the great machine be exerted.

In regard to the intrinsic value of the great man as creator and to his capabilities as reformer, Balzac again manifests an ambivalent outlook. His idealism, which makes him hope fervently for the success of the great man, is constantly befogged by his realism, which uncovers the vulnerability of the genius-reformer.

The first and most obvious difficulty lies in the relationship between the great man and a society made up of mediocre, money-hungry people. How the latter accept this aristocrat of the mind is described in the *Album.* "The superiority of the masses renders the greatness of the individual more difficult."[15] It has already been demonstrated that weakness is automatically rejected because it does not fit into the utilitarian demands of the societal structure. It stands to reason then that the different and the incongruous will be rejected in the same manner and for the same reason. This is the discovery of Benassis, the great man who flees from society in order to mold a perfect community after his own fashion.

> Horrible epoch, when one must bend down before a po-
> lite, mediocre and cold man whom one hates, but whom
> one must obey. I discovered later the reasons for these
> apparent inconsistencies. Mediocrity, sir, suffices for all

15. Ibid., p. 28.

the hours of life; it is the daily clothing of society; everything which extends beyond the sweet shadow projected
by mediocre people is too glittering; genius and originality
are jewels which one locks away and keeps to be worn on
certain days. (*Le Médecin de campagne, 8,* 488–89)

That which the great man has to offer mankind is somehow
unacceptable to the very nature of the human situation and
therefore ignored or misunderstood. The gifts of genius and the
fruits of talent are luxuries, abhorred by all who are common.

In rebuttal, one can point to the utopian visions of *Le Médecin
de campagne* and *Le Curé de village.* These novels offer proofs
of Balzac's belief in the perfectibility of the masses. Their
visions are utopian, and therein lies their fallacy. The reforms
wrought by Benassis and Véronique Graslin are miracles performed with a magician's wand. There are no setbacks, no
natural catastrophes that interfere with the formula for instant
progress prescribed by Balzac. It is also interesting to note that
both of these experiments take place in mountain villages, cut
off from the world, from reality. What happens when the reformer tries to benefit a population that is not insulated, where
his equals are not enlightened lawyers and saintly curates? The
answer lies in *Les Paysans.* There we see the high-minded prop-
erty owner who, in his desire to institute land reforms that will
help the peasants, is finally driven from his own land. He is
opposed by the very people he seeks to benefit, and these people
are led in their opposition by unscrupulous magistrates. The
old general's one sin is a sense of superiority.

> Note that this league made up of an entire canton and of
> a small city against an old general who escaped the dangers
> of a thousand combats in spite of his courage, has been
> formed in more than one district against men who wanted
> to do good there. This coalition incessantly menaces the
> man of genius, the great politician, the great agronomist,
> and finally all innovators. (*Les Paysans, 8,* 154)

The elegiac portions of *Le Médecin de campagne* and *Le Curé de village*, which deal with the successful efforts of reform, have something of the romantic idealism of *Jocelyn*. They have the quality of a fable, quite antithetical to Balzac's usual tone, which he uses to describe a world decidedly unromantic and not in the least bit utopian. No well-intentioned institution that the world has created can allow idealism to exist, because idealism, however futile, troubles the course of all-powerful mediocrity.

> If government had a thought, I would suspect it of being afraid of truly superior people who, once awakened, would put society under the yoke of an intelligent power. Since nations would then go too far too quickly, the professors are ordered to shape blockheads. How can we otherwise explain a teaching profession without method, without plan for the future? (*Louis Lambert, 10, 412*)

Balzac returns again and again to the idiotic paradox that dooms reform, morality, and ideals. The impulse in man to create systems of government, of justice, of dogma that will regulate his baser desires is checked by the cunning with which the baser desires finally bend the systems. In the end, the natural human thirsts find ways to satiate themselves. Society refuses to train talent properly; the fate of Z. Marcas demonstrates that it does not reward disinterested idealism. And society's attitude toward pure genius is even more unmerciful.

> Men appear to have even more respect for vices than for Genius, for they refuse to give it credit. It seems that the profits gained from the secret labors of the scholar are so distant that the social organism fears dealing with him during his lifetime, and prefers getting out of its obligation by not pardoning him his misery or his misfortunes. (*La Recherche de l'absolu, 9, 489*)

Since the immediate fruits of genius are intangible, have no market value, cannot be bought or sold, they are despised by an ignorant, materialistic society.

Thus far, Balzac has raised an accusing finger against society, labeling it the cause for the failure of the genius-reformer. But the author's deep-grained sense of relativity shows him that this failure has manifold roots that lie hidden in the very nature of the genius. The genius possesses, and must by definition possess, certain qualities that make him not only unfit to benefit society, but even incapable of living in it. Balzac realizes that the traits that consitute genius, the special gift of vision and comprehension, the highly developed involvement with absolutes of beauty and truth, push the genius so far out of the daily living context that he is no longer able to deal with it effectively. Artistic perception is often incompatible with business acumen and with the practicality demanded by the mere fact of living in the world and dealing with its banal problems. Balzac sees in those fictional characters who pass for men of great talent a discouraging lack of common sense, an inability to judge life's realities at close range, and a blindness to the truth of their own personalities. "Why this lack of penetration into their personal affairs in men accustomed to penetrate everything? Perhaps the mind cannot be complete in all of its aspects, perhaps artists live too much in the present to study the future" (*Une Fille d'Eve,* 2, 138). This ignorance of the workings of practical life is a crippling infirmity to the exalted spirit of the genius. He who is thus afflicted is prevented from helping others and, often, from helping himself.

But even if the genius were able to judge reality correctly, he would not be saved from doom. A comprehension of society's injustice may teach him to abandon his idealistic way of life and thereby jeopardize the very thing that makes him a special member of the human community. If he decides to compromise his principles he can always justify it as an act of self-defense. Benassis, Balzac's country doctor, is a particularly acute observer of this process. "The continuous tableau of happy vice and bantered virtue imperceptibly shakes a young man; Parisian life soon takes the down off his conscience; then begins and ends the hellish job of his demoralization" (*Le Médecin de campagne, 8,* 477). The brutal realism of Balzac's logic stands out clearly in this passage. The qualities that he prizes most, the pure intelligence and sensitivity of the young man, are piteously sacrificed to the callous corruption that characterizes modern society. The author unflinchingly shows that a possible awareness of the realities of life, which is produced by this very intelligence and sensitivity, leaves the man of talent little choice. He must join in the struggle for existence and assume all the compromises that this choice implies, or forever be an outcast. He does not even have the comfort of seeing that the outcast enjoys any particular reward. This produces the bitter realization that the tempo and the values of mediocrity are favored by the world and that he who remains out of step with this tempo or discordant to these values must inevitably be crushed. The artist or thinker is forced to play two games at the same time, and as a result, he often plays neither of them very well. He is torn between the demands of the real world and those of the ideal. The material desires and the intellectual purity that these two worlds generate are uneasy companions when lodged within the same spirit. Thus, the artist is doomed to fail. He cannot please both poles that govern his existence.

There are other factors that serve to undermine the myth of the great man. Balzac knows that a superior character is not necessarily linked to a great mind. The development of intellectual genius is no guarantee that a genius for morality, a capacity for goodness, and a spirit of charity are concomitants. In fact, "It is extremely rare to find harmony between talent and character" (*Modeste Mignon, 1,* 406–07). Thus, the author loses much of his faith in the genius-reformer, the man who is above human baseness and who, as a specially gifted seer, will regulate the ways of other men in order to perfect society.

Why does Balzac insist upon this separation between the faculties of creative genius and moral judgment? For one aspect of the explanation we must look to the famous *ange* of Swedenborg, in whose ethereal but perceptible existence Balzac

firmly believes.[16] The *ange* is that purest part of the human
being in communion with the celestial. It is a human element
unrelated to the creative intelligence. The *ange* is the spirit of
absolute goodness, which may exist in the simplest of men, for
this goodness is a gift from a divine force, unbound by earthly
standards and by intellectual considerations. Thus, the genius,
upon whom the gift of goodness is, one may assume, not necessarily bestowed, remains very much a man. He must, by definition, submit to the pressures and the forces that coerce and
pervert other men. The genius is therefore left with a single
weapon, a highly developed intellect, which does not automatically equip one to fight for the cause of good, truth, and justice.

There is still another dangerous aspect to a superabundance
of intelligence. A concentration of this mental force by a process
of transference will possibly, and even probably, breed a parallel
concentration of the demand for pleasure. Once again, Balzac
perceives that the great man is doomed to failure, this time
because he may demand great and ruining distractions. "Gen-
erals, ministers, artists are more or less drawn toward dissolution by the need to oppose violent distractions to their existence
so far removed from common life" (*La Peau de chagrin, 9,* 150).

Balzac, not content to point out the pressures that the world
exerts on the artist or the human fallibility of the genius,
searches deeper and finds a terrible flaw in the thought process
itself. He is convinced that an overactive functioning of the
intelligence leads to a total loss of perspective and eventual
madness. Since the concentration of an idea gives the idea undue
proportions, it invades the mind and destroys the judgment
necessary for living. This concept is the guiding motive in
"Études philosophiques." In his introduction to this collection,
Philarète Chasles faithfully describes Balzac's intention. "Analysis, the last development of thought, has thus killed the plea-

16. For a particularly lucid account of mysticism in Balzac see Laubriet,
L'Intelligence de l'art, pp. 287–303.

sures of thought. It is what M. de Balzac has seen in his time, it is the final result of that axiom of Jean-Jacques: The man who thinks is a depraved animal" (Introduction aux "Romans et contes philosophiques," *11, 181*). Throughout *La Comédie humaine* there are examples of artists and thinkers who completely lose contact with reality and partake of the fruits of another world, a world of ideals and ideas. They become unnaturally obsessed by an *idée fixe*. It has already been illustrated that the author regretfully admits the failure of ideals and ideas in coping with reality. Thus, the genius is cut loose from the world, a monster of thought rejected by the machine. And there is one final, unhappy paradox. The overdevelopment of thought kills the object upon which the thought is focused. The author writes:

> *Massimilla Doni, Gambara, Le Chef-d'oeuvre inconnu,* then *La Frélore,* another "Étude philosophique" published in a review, and *Les Deux sculpteurs,* which will be published soon without a doubt, are works which continue, in a way, *La Peau de chagrin.* They show the disorder produced in the soul of the artist by thought completely developed; they demonstrate the laws which produce the suicide of art. (Préface d'*Une Fille d'Eve, 11,* 380)

But the sentence that Balzac has just pronounced on the excesses of thought does not appear sufficiently harsh to him. The concentration of thought produces not only the suicide of art, but the suicide of the artist, the suicide of the man. Claës and Gambara are horribly degraded; Frenhofer burns himself alive; Louis Lambert goes mad attempting to castrate himself. This is not a happy record in favor of the contemplative or creative life. Balzac finally labels as pernicious the very characteristic that distinguishes the human species from the animal. He sees a fallacy in man's very humanity, defining this in his article, "Théorie de la démarche": "Thus, thought is the power which corrupts our movement, which twists our bodies, which makes them burst under its despotic efforts. It is the great solvent of the human species."[17]

In these statements of attitude and purpose it is obvious that Balzac has completely stripped idealism and optimism from his definition of the world. He leaves the reader a construct in which these qualities are flaws in individuals and nonentities in institutions. Balzac has not let himself be carried away by his natural sentimentality, his romantic belief in the perfectibility of man. That the masses are perfectible in his pastoral test cases has no relevance in the reality of the universe he posits. One thus returns to the great machine with its basic laws. He who functions well in relation to the machine will succeed; he who mistakenly looks to other systems for order will fail. The great lesson that the Balzacian character learns is the lesson of expediency, for expediency is the only watchword that will help him through life. He must bend his intelligence to this end as a guard against unpragmatic idealism and, therefore, an unhealthy functioning of this very intelligence. A man's only hope is his clear realization that the world is governed by mechanistic principles, that nothing succeeds like success, and that this success is measured by money. Gobseck expresses this in a succinct credo. "Is not life a machine whose rhythm is set by money? Know this, the means are always confused with the ends: you will never succeed in separating the soul from the senses, spirit from matter. Gold is the spiritualism of your present societies" (*Gobseck*, 2, 636). With this philosophy in mind one is at least not handicapped in the mad race for success. Balzac preaches this pragmatism throughout *La Comédie*

17. Balzac, "Théorie de la démarche," *Oeuvres complètes*, édition Bouteron (Paris, 1938), 39, 640. This article first appeared in *L'Europe littéraire* on August 5, 18, 25, and September 5, 1833. According to a catalogue attached to the second volume of "Un Grand homme de province à Paris" in 1839, Balzac intended to include it in *Pathologie de la vie sociale*, a work he never completed.

humaine. Success, or the avoidance of failure, depends on the ability of the individual to judge the ways of the world and act according to the demands of the given situation. The unfolding of the situation is brought about by the intricate byplay of natural forces and the self-interest of individuals, and it must be confronted with lucidity and dealt with as unscrupulously as the events merit. In the various success stories found in the novels one searches in vain for a word about morality, consideration for the other man, truth, loyalty, love. Penetrating vision, concentration of force and will, and quick judgment count in the vicious struggle for existence that rages in the world. In the light of Balzac's peculiarly developed views about the conservation of energy, this sort of foresight has an obvious priority. Men must follow the example of the long-distance runner who keeps a steady pace, only to burst ahead at the all-important climax.

This husbanding of energy is controlled by foresight, a literally penetrating vision in Balzacian terms. But there are other things that the successful man sees and that the failure obviously does not comprehend. He realizes that in an amoral world, corruption is a tool he must and should use in charting his life's direction. Vautrin gives this sage advice to Rastignac. Through default of a special brand of evil genius, the kind that Vautrin himself possesses, one must plunge headlong into the swarm of struggling men and struggle there more vigorously and with less principle than the others. "Honesty serves no purpose. . . . Corruption dominates, talent is rare. Thus corruption is the weapon of the mediocrity which abounds, and you will feel its point everywhere" (*Le Père Goriot, 2,* 936). The world here in question rejects the type of genius personified in Louis Lambert by the same impulse with which it rejects the ineptitude of César Birotteau. The genius' interests are so far from earthly matters that he has no chance of being noticed in a worldly context; the poor perfumer, condemned to the struggle for survival, refuses to find strength for this struggle in the practical corruption rampant in his sphere. Neither of these characters is able to adapt himself to the exigencies of the moment, the life experience with its unpretty truths and immense challenge. It would mean compromising, in one case, intellectual ideals, in the other, moral ones. Such luxuries are not permitted by a society that has made such cheap coin of dishonesty. Vautrin predicts success for the genius who devotes his gifts to the task of making a way for himself in the world, and for the mediocre man who does not hesitate to sacrifice scruples for personal gain. They both are free to fight and therefore have a chance to succeed. At least they and their opponents occupy the same arena.

The true test of the successful man lies in his ability to reject his own passions, ignore his predilections, and rid himself of poetic chimeras. He must keep his vision absolutely clear and, to do so, must concentrate all his energy to that end. In his *Album,* Balzac paints a dreadful portrait of just such a being. "The cold man discusses, the passionate man acts, one has lymph and the other blood. A cold man who acts is terrifying."[18] This brand of coldness involves the sacrifice of pleasures and hopes and demands unwavering devotion to the dissection of reality with the finely honed instrument that is an unclouded judgment. "For a young man it suffices to meet a woman who does not love him, or a woman who loves him too much, so that his whole life is upset. Happiness swallows up our strength, just as misfortune extinguishes our virtues" (*La Peau de chagrin, 9,* 147). Nothing is so fatal to the progress of the ambitious man as the numbing complacency of happiness and the debilitating expenditure of passions. These are traps laid by the weak side of human nature, the side which is least compatible with the machinelike organism that is the world. "Happy he who has never been happy."[19] This aphorism may be interpreted realistically as well as romantically. It takes on a special meaning when viewed in relationship to the joyless program of conduct

18. Balzac, *Pensées,* p. 22.
19. Ibid., p. 12.

that the author presents to the man with aspirations. A success must do all that he can to de-emphasize those aspects of his personality that crave happiness and pleasure, the true harbingers of failure. He must have thorough command of himself so that he can present to the moment the visage it demands. "The fact is thus no longer anything in itself, it is entirely in the idea that others have of it. From that, young man, a second precept: have a beautiful exterior, hide the underside of your life, and present a very brilliant surface!" (*Illusions perdues, 4,* 1024) Since the world judges only what it sees, that which is exterior, the inner life and the real personality which lie beneath the shell of expediency one is commanded to wear are useless. At best, this inner life will be a source of torment, for it will always be a sign that uncompromised ideals lost the battle to pragmatic amorality.

The inner life, composed of passions, pleasures, and dreams, has still another drawback. Its presence implies that one relies on a rigid, personalized system for dealing with events. This is a grave egotistical miscalculation. The man who is a slave to himself is unable to fashion a mask suitable to the particular circumstance facing him. He is hampered by preconceived notions, by considerations that subvert his judgment and prevent a dispassionate appraisal of reality. He is laden down with a useless appendage—a personality. He will fail like the actor who is unable to transfigure his own particular ego and present a convincing image to his audience. In a world of more or less accomplished actors, one must don an effective mask or else be hooted off the stage.

Little is left to the successful man. He has voided himself of illusions, ideals, desires, passions, and personality. He is an empty shell, scarcely human. This is the alternative to self-destruction in the struggle for existence. On the one hand, Balzac offers crippling distortion and death. "Thus the excessive activity of the proletariat, the depravation of interest which pulverizes the two bourgeoisies, the cruelties of artistic thought, and the excesses of pleasure incessantly sought by the great, explain the normal ugliness of the Parisian face" (*La Fille aux yeux d'or*, 5, 268). On the other hand, a complete renunciation of what Balzac calls the goddess Necessity produces a soulless, desireless shell, a semi-dead man. The pessimism of an author who reaches such an impasse is poignant and particularly convincing.

La Comédie humaine, however, is not an impasse, for it charts the fascinating paths that lead to failure or success as measured by the eyes of the world. It becomes obvious that a character's destiny depends entirely upon the application of the rule of expediency to the situation of the moment. As Louis Lambert says, "Here, everything must have an immediate, real result" (*Louis Lambert*, 10, 411). For a novelist who sets himself the task of reporting a moment in history, a task that involves minute observation of the many sides of this moment, the creative process is greatly akin to the lucidity of the successful man. Balzac sees the machine in action and deduces the conduct of a variety of men in relation to the machine. This deduction, made by the individual for himself, is the secret of success. It can be achieved only by the utilization of a cold-blooded, realistic view, an honest and true appraisal of one's talents and defects, and the sober knowledge that the world is neither good nor bad; it simply is. Félix Davin succinctly defines Balzac's objectivity.

> His unity had to be the world, man was only the detail. He proposed to paint him in all of life's circumstances, to describe him in all his aspects, to seize him in all his phases, important and inconsequential, neither completely good, nor completely vicious, struggling with laws in his own interests, struggling with morals because of his own feelings, logical or great by chance. He wanted to show society ceaselessly dissolved, ceaselessly recomposed, men-

acing because it is menaced, he wanted to finally achieve
the design of its totality by reconstructing, one by one, its
elements. (Introduction aux "Études de moeurs," *11*, 230)

The fact that Balzac or the Balzacian hero may have notions
of good and bad, truth and mendacity, has nothing to do with
their vision of the world. The world they both depend on is
basically immutable. It is difficult enough to see it and adapt
to it. Failure measured by the standards of this world, that is
the lack of money, esteem, and power, is caused by an imperfect
adjustment to the great machine, and the variations that this
imperfect adjustment assumes in *La Comédie humaine* provides
for the variety of the novels. Balzac describes the tensions that
exist between the talents and liabilities of the individual and
the path he chooses for himself. Very often, this path is not
the one he is meant to choose. It is when the way of the world
demands one course of action, and the character opts for another,
that failure is decreed.

CHAPTER 2

The Blind: Comic Hyperbole

According to Balzac, ruthless judgment, exercised with the perspicacity of a Vautrin, is necessary not only for success, but simply for survival. The sin of the blind man lies in his lack of congruity with the needs of reality, in his unwillingness to rid himself of useless ideals such as probity and trust, and especially, in his ignorance of the constant flow of deception that governs the actions of his opponents. Doomed to function in the cloud that is his mistaken assessment of life, the blind man fumbles toward his failure in *La Comédie humaine* with the same relentlessness that characterizes the other figures in Balzac's gallery of *ratés*.

The author is pitiless as he condemns these poor, silly men to their destruction with no tearful regrets. In recounting this type of failure, Balzac neither spares nor pampers the reader by mitigating the succession of details that points to the character's stupidity, to his lack of comprehension, to his comical self-damnation through ignorance. In the stories of the brothers Birotteau and Paul de Manerville, the three most memorable *ingénus* in *La Comédie humaine,* one feels the author exulting in his own superiority. In spite of the fact that they are pleasant, affectionate, and attractive people, their dreadful incapacity for decisive and effective action inspires pity neither from the author nor from the reader. So strong and awesome is the mechanism of the universe, a mechanism worthy of challenge, that the ignorant refusal to take on this challenge does not merit compassion. The exciting current of will that charges through the pages of *La Comédie humaine* and is the unifying force within this gigantic literary corpus elicits the reader's most fervent approbation. It is the factor that reflects Balzac's humanism, his conviction that human energy knows no bounds. While he does not exactly show contempt for Birotteau the perfumer, Birotteau the priest, and Paul de Manerville, the aristocrat hero of *Le Contrat de mariage,* his portraits contain more than a little disdain for these characters, as they so meekly succumb to their destinies. Through the betrayal of their true humanity, the trust imposed upon them to struggle, they relinquish all right to pity.

Of special interest is the mode adopted by the author in the presentation of his complex point of view. He has set himself the difficult task of describing heroes who are shorn of all traditionally heroic qualities and of constructing novels that can successfully revolve around such unusual protagonists. Furthermore, these characters have none of the glamor found in the most unheroic of romantic and existentialist figures. They are simply stupid men. Balzac's problem is, therefore, to find a way of couching this stupidity in such a way that it will fascinate his readers. The method he chooses is an unqualified success and one of his most original contributions to the range of novelistic expression. It is the injection of comic hyperbole into the ultraserious fabric of *La Comédie humaine.* Hints of this technique, for example, Lucien de Rubempré's suicide note in *Illusions perdues,* are expanded and establish the tonality for novels like *César Birotteau, Le Curé de Tours,* and *Le Contrat de mariage.* Thus, Balzac finds another way of varying his presentation of the ways of the world. In doing so, he gives an extra dimension to his fiction, a body of novels so vast that the author is constantly faced with the risk of excessive repetition. This new dimension has a life-giving quality, for its effect is jarring and shocking. Balzac's reader knows that the world is a tragic place, and to encounter the comic therein, even though it may be a grim, macabre, or cruel comic, is an unsettling experience. This reaction is exactly the one that the author seeks to evoke. In his effort to impart awareness, he often resorts to the technique of shocking incongruence. The reader's first reaction is to wonder at the appearance of comedy in this serious indictment of life, and yet, at the very moment of wonder, the author's intention becomes apparent and his message conveyed. He has successfully elicited attention. We read these novels in a state of uneasy excitement, anxious to discover how the comic heroes will be touched by the constantly menacing world and made uncomfortable by the inevitable scenes of painful contact.

Balzac does not, for a moment, consider the plight of the Birotteau brothers or Paul de Manerville comic. No man's plight is comic in the eyes of this author who sees all of reality's impossible ramifications. For him, the comic is merely a literary device. In order to avoid transgressing the consistency of his literary world he chooses a brand of comedy that emanates directly from the characters. It is a comedy tuned by the relationship between these men and their aspirations, by the breach between their true stature and the mold to which they should wittingly or unwittingly conform. The distance separating the fact of their lives and the fiction of their dreams offers a rich source for the author's repertoire of comic hyperbole. Time and again, he places over an objectively detailed description of the hero's shortcomings a projection of his absent strength or the shadow of a superior opponent. The hero is eternally unaware of his deficiencies, and his blissful, and sometimes not so blissful, ignorance is unfailingly comic. Balzac succeeds in wringing a score of permutations from one basic comic situation. The lamb enters the lion's den, expects to be invited to dinner, and inevitably, unavoidably is devoured.

Balzac never attempts to disguise his intention. In the story of César Birotteau, he gives away his comic point of view in the novel's title: *Histoire de la grandeur et de la décadence de César Birotteau, marchand parfumeur, adjoint au maire du deuxième arrondissement de Paris, chevalier de la Légion d'honneur.* This monster of a title belongs to that category of reliable and perfectly obvious signals that the author insists on giving his reader, directing him to the profoundest realization of his fiction's complexities. The title is a mine of information, which Balzac is determined to impart before the slightest ambiguity can trouble the reader's comprehension. The importance of this integral element in the author's aesthetics cannot be stressed too strongly. The title describes the rhythm of the novel, explains the reasons for the hero's failure, and sets the tone of comic hyperbole. Its very length is a clue to the fact that Balzac does not have the utmost reverence for César Birotteau. It seems to be the title of a mock heroic, where inflated high style is used to point up the smallness of the subject.[1] Its rhetorical amplitude seems fitting for the history of nations, of kings, of great men. But who is César Birotteau? Although his life can rightly claim both the author's and reader's attention, his rise and fall are hardly worthy of the title's majesty.

The various appellations that Balzac bestows upon Birotteau are another source of amusement and another insight into the purpose of the novel. The priority given to *marchand parfumeur* prepares us for the discovery that this is the character's main occupation, and given the modest nature of this profession, one wonders at the appropriateness of the two succeeding roles ascribed to the hero. The honest peasant who comes to Paris with only a few coins in his pocket has neither the intelligence nor the temperament to be a judge, and the reference to the Legion of Honor contributes an additional comic slant.

The elephantiasis of the title suggests the fumblings, aspira-

1. The comic qualities of this title are noted by Raymond Giraud in *The Unheroic Hero in the Novels of Stendhal, Balzac and Flaubert* (New Brunswick, 1957), p. 102, and by Harry Levin in *The Gates of Horn* (New York, 1963), p. 155.

tions, and foibles of César Birotteau. Readers acquainted with Balzac's rigid theories about species, about the importance of congruity between the individual's capacities and functions, will not be surprised that César Birotteau's story ends in what the author terms *décadence*. The hero can at best be a perfume salesman. As he attempts to change his lot, as he misjudges his abilities and aims for a success beyond his reach, he dooms himself to failure. César Birotteau refuses to pay heed to the voice of his own personality, in which he should hear the echo of his potential. Instead of using these indications and thus skillfully planning his life, he blindly gropes his way in terrains to which he has no right of entry and eagerly grasps the hands of two-faced enemies. The *marchand parfumeur* becomes inept once he steps over the sill of his shop. Unfit by nature to enjoy any degree of *grandeur*, it is inevitable that he will stumble headlong into a precipitous *décadence*. Balzac wishes to emphasize the fact that this novel is to be a description of failure; the very word, *décadence*, looms up behind each event, each decision made by the hero, each of his small and deceptive triumphs. Balzac has added still another element to the monolithic background of the novel. As it takes its place in *La Comédie humaine*, following the prefaces, pronouncements, and previous case histories, *César Birotteau* fits neatly into the web of determinism woven by the author's omniscient imagination. The reader versed in the bylaws of the Balzacian universe shares the author's omniscience. But for the uninitiated, the author conveniently supplies the word *décadence*, thus permitting him to follow the hero's destiny without surprise, armed with the knowledge of imminent doom.

In the novel's first scene Balzac continues to plot the hero's defeat by providing explicit prefigurations. The prophetic dream of Madame Birotteau, upon which the novel opens, is not to any degree comic and therefore lies outside the province of this discussion. The couple's subsequent conversation, as revealing as the dream, is a prime example of the author's comic style. Its position is in itself comic, as it follows the macabre seriousness used to recount Madame Birotteau's premonition. The contrast between César's shopkeeper's voice and the awesome extent of the fate awaiting him indicates the disproportion between his true stature and the magnificence of his aspirations. "Aren't there vinegar-makers, mustard merchants who command the National Guard, and who are very well considered at the Château? Let's imitate them, expand our business interests, and at the same time let's push ourselves into high society" (*César Birotteau*, 5, 330). Birotteau fails to see the humor in the vinegar, mustard, and perfume invasion of high society. For him, anything is possible, and in his ingenuous belief in limitless possibility lies the fundamental chord of the author's comic hyperbole. Madame Birotteau attempts to puncture her husband's glossy balloon with her sharp tongue.

> "Look, Birotteau, do you know what I think when I listen to you? Well, you're like a man looking for a needle in a haystack. Remember what I told you when there was talk of your becoming mayor: your peace of mind above all! I said to you, 'You are cut out to be in the public eye like my arm is to be a mill vane. Greatness will be your undoing.'" (ibid., p. 330)

The tone of this exchange, with its common sense and homely humor, considerably tempers the *grandeur* suggested by the title. The flat-footed crack made by Madame Birotteau aptly indicates her mentality, fills in her characterization, and demonstrates the incongruence of César and his aspirations. The distance between Madame Birotteau's arm and the peaks of the Parisian business arena is epic in its hilarity and eloquence.

The persistent humor in the first part of the novel is fraught with expectancy, as we wait for César to slip on the proverbial banana peel. The world he is about to enter is one that must reject him. Balzac capitalizes upon this inevitability, constantly ridiculing the poor perfumer and thereby increasing the reader's apprehension over the coming fall. His previous success was based on his probity, momentary blindness on the part of the world at large, and chance. As his horizons widen, none of these factors will come to his rescue. It is, in fact, these new horizons that describe the comic framework for his small personality and small intelligence.

> Contrary to appearances, the merchant was timid, while his wife had patience and courage. Thus a cowardly, mediocre man, without education, without ideas, without acquaintances, without character, who was not to succeed in the most precarious spot in the world, through his spirit of good conduct, through his feeling for justice, through the goodness of a soul truly Christian, through love for the only woman he had possessed, succeeded in passing for a remarkable, courageous and resolute man. (ibid., p. 357)

The public will not be fooled much longer, for the quality of the public has changed, and the stakes are much higher. César Birotteau is a midget masquerading as a giant, and the gradual demasking process is both sad and funny.

Balzac never fails to exploit the cock-eyed proportions running through the novel. He makes striking use of this method in the confrontation between Birotteau and his adversary, Du Tillet. The extent of their dissemblance is to be expected from an author who delights in such pairings.[2] The strange coupling of Birotteau and his former employee has humorously exaggerated overtones. They are indeed mismatched, and the foolishness of Birotteau's struggle can be read in his opponent's eyes.

> His sly face was pleasing on first sight; but later, upon knowing him better, one perceived those strange expressions that are painted on the visage of people ill at ease

---

2. See Gaëton Picon, *Balzac par lui-même* (Paris, 1956), pp. 109–36, for an interesting discussion of the pairing mechanism in Balzac.

48

with themselves, or whose conscience is wont to grumble.
. . . The look of those multi-colored eyes encased in a sheet
of silver was fleeting, but terrible when he riveted it directly upon his victim. (ibid., p. 359)

The face and eyes of Birotteau are pathetic indications that he
does not stand the slightest chance against the machinations of
Du Tillet. The contrast is ludicrous and faithful to the current
of comic hyperbole unleashed in the novel's title. "His forehead
. . . reflected the simplicity of his life. His thick eyebrows were
hardly frightening, for his blue eyes, through their limpid,
ever-frank glance, harmonized with his honest man's forehead"
(ibid., pp. 363–64). Birotteau will not find his open face and
his good heart particularly effective assets as he struggles for
existence. The struggle, so often defined by the confrontation
of eyes in *La Comédie humaine,* is between foes of absurdly
unequal capacities.

    This brand of disproportion casts a comic light upon César's
brother in *Le Curé de Tours.* Their faces express the same
naïveté; they are guileless. Their respective adversaries, of
course, manifest the inscrutibility essential in successful, and
therefore necessarily ruthless, men. The malice of Du Tillet is
precisely foreshadowed in the face of Abbé Troubert.

    It was impossible to find two faces which offered as many
    contrasts as the ones presented by those of the two abbés.
    Troubert, tall and dried out, had a yellow and bilious
    complexion, while the vicar was what one familiarly calls
    chubby. Round and reddish, Birotteau's face betrayed a
    thoughtless good nature; that of Troubert, long and fur-
    rowed with deep wrinkles, acquired, at times, an expres-
    sion full of irony or disdain. But one needed to examine
    it with attention in order to discover those two sentiments.
    (*Le Curé de Tours, 3,* 803)

In this humorous diptych the author draws from the comparison an adjunct to the portrait. Obviously, Troubert's characteristics are made clearer when seen in conjunction with those of Birotteau. The concision of the description, in keeping with the brevity of the novel, is made possible by the way these characters play against each other. Troubert in particular profits from this technique. It is in the nature of the mystery surrounding him that his force be presented obliquely, by implication, by possibility. The scope of his domination over Birotteau and, by extension, over Tours is comic in the disparity of the match and in the reasons for the opposition. In this short novel the author's grasp of the mock heroic is striking.

The process of comic hyperbole, particularly in "Scènes de la vie de province," springs from the very nature of his subject. Balzac has set himself the task of describing small lives, lives that are bound by small conventions, whose goals, joys, and even sorrows are small. This is unusual fictional matter and it demands an unusual approach. Twenty years prior to Balzac, no one would have considered the Birotteau brothers fitting heroes for a novel, much less a serious novel. The author, however, is convinced that any life is worthy of investigation; at the same time he is aware of the artistic problems presented by such an assumption. He must choose a framework that is arresting yet capable of setting off the minature lives in question without betraying their dimensions. The traditional mold of the mock heroic is a convenient one. The story of Abbé Birotteau shows the extent to which Balzac can treat, in a pseudo-epic tone, the story of a man both intellectually and emotionally impoverished. The meticulous description of his return to Mademoiselle Gamard's pension, on a rainy autumn night, details, without an audible snicker from the author, the hero's mundane perplexities.

Then, as the nature of narrow-minded people brings them to understand minutia, he gave himself suddenly to great

reflections upon these four events, imperceptible to anyone
else, but which, for him, constituted four catastrophes.
Evidently the entire loss of his happiness was involved in
the forgetting of his slippers, in Marianne's lie concerning
the fire, in the unusual transfer of his candle from the table
of the anti-chamber, and in the wait in the rain, on the
doorsill, that they had engineered for him. (ibid., p. 792)

In the life of the curate of Tours these four events do most
emphatically constitute catastrophes. They are major domestic
tragedies, the only kind the ignorant man can recognize. Birotteau's outlandish reaction sets off a series of impressions within
the reader. The first is one of frank amusement, elicited by the
character's tone of exaggerated seriousness. The language controls the comic aspect of the hyperbole and serves to focus the
reader's attention. This is immediately followed by the realization that the character is not in the least exaggerating, and
that in terms of his existence, the tone of his despair is not
unwarranted. The more awesome realization of the curate's
inability to perceive real tragedy, blinded as he is by the misfortunes of the *foyer,* comes close behind. One cannot forget
the silly, fat man, wailing about his drenched moment on the
doorsill, as he blithely strolls into the infernal plot unleashed
by Troubert, a plot bounded by mediocrity—the cupidity of
Birotteau, the petty pride of Mademoiselle Gamard, an apartment, a candle. But upon finishing the novel, one is left with
the image of Troubert, that Innocent III, that Peter the Great,
who lurks in the cloister of Saint-Gatien. He is power; he is
reality; he is the mass of universal forces against which is
pitted the miniscule existence of Birotteau. It is evident that
a matter-of-fact tone will not do justice to the comic qualities
of Birotteau's immediate situation or to the serious qualities
implied by his life's predicament. Balzac makes a wise choice
in adopting an epic tone, for it at once deflates the importance of
Birotteau as an individual and is eminently suited to locate his

great importance in the framework of *La Comédie humaine*. Through the use of comic disproportion the author can remain faithful to his two principal goals, a suitable artistic represen- tation of trivia and a proper vehicle for his lofty ambition.

The comic has a deep resonance in these novels and succeeds in eliciting a variety of impressions. Dramatizing the now- familiar theme of disproportion between the blind character's self-awareness and the true extent of his failure, the curate of Tours never understands the reasons for his doom as he stares dumbly at life from the porch of his modest parish. César Birotteau is similarly deprived of real cognizance of the events and forces that cause his ruin. While his financial world is chipped away by rapid strokes, Birotteau continues to struggle with his illusions, seeking to salvage the unsalvageable, re- fusing to believe that, in spite of his probity, he will fail. With the final dim realization that the business world has deceived him, his existence is shattered. But even this realization is comic in its manifestation, because the remedy sought by Birotteau is totally unrelated to his failure.

> César, illuminated by this fatal and last ray of light, finally saw the awful truth in all its dimensions. He fell back on the easy-chair, from there to his knees, his reason left him, he became a child again. His wife thought he was dying, she kneeled down to pick him up; but she copied him when she saw him join his hands, raise his eyes and recite with resigned solemnity the sublime prayer of the Catholics, in the presence of his uncle, his daughter and Popinot. (*César Birotteau, 5,* 534)

A madman, a child, a pater noster are poor relics to replace the once ambitious *marchand parfumeur*. The recital of the prayer is a foolish gesture, a joke in a system that scorns emotion, belief, and sincerity. Birotteau, in his semi-ignorant desolation, instinc- tively turns to his principles, the principles that have conspired

to doom him. He makes the prayer offering into a public utterance, as if to reaffirm somehow his belief in goodness and to
salvage meaning from his previous existence. The pater noster,
in its comic inappropriateness, accentuates the distance between
Birotteau's resources and those demanded by the ruthless world
of speculation. It is an empty prayer, invoking a god who has
no authority over real estate profiteers.

César Birotteau then sets out to restore his reputation and
pay his debts. He is capable of this small challenge because it
demands only his perseverance. But although he achieves a
symbol of success at the end of the story, recognition for his
honesty, he has actually failed in his life's most significant
endeavor. The one time he gambles in the game of high ambition he loses. His final apotheosis is actually a return to his
position at the beginning of the novel.

How is one to explain the glorious apotheosis at the end of
César Birotteau? One seems urged to interpret the hero's death
to the celestial harmonies of a Beethoven symphony as a fitting
end for a life of probity and hard work. "This ideal music
radiated, sparkled in every mode, sounded its bugles in the
meninx of this exhausted brain, for which it was to be the
grand finale" (ibid., p. 590). Birotteau succumbs from emotion
upon realizing that his reputatiton has been restored. He dies
hearing the music that accompanied his exultation at the ball
which climaxes the first part of the novel. Ironically, this ball,
the symbol of Birotteau's folly, plays an important role in his
financial failure. No less ironically, all his unsuspected enemies
were invited. Nonetheless, it is here that he first hears, in his
mind's ear, the finale of the Beethoven symphony, the music
that is the sonic equivalent of his unbounded joy, his flight to
a sphere of happiness and perfection. In the last sentence of
the novel, Balzac properly beatifies Birotteau. "Jesus ordered
the Earth to render its prey, the holy priest showed Heaven a
martyr to commercial probity to be decorated with the eternal
palm" (ibid., p. 591). Birotteau is a martyr for a most unworthy

cause, and the palm with which he is decorated is the final sign
of his failure. It is awarded for a concept, while the world in
which he fails is totally governed by fact.

The musical finale is a particularly savage bit of comedy
injected into the novel. César Birotteau is perfectly incapable
of appreciating Beethoven. His life is strictly confined to his
perfume shop and to his love for his wife and daughter. He does
not have the capacity for other emotions; he cannot perceive
other horizons. While Birotteau dumbly hears the music of
Beethoven, Balzac proceeds to describe, in extravagantly romantic terms, the aesthetic experience offered by such music.

> A radiant fairy emerges raising her wand. You hear the
> rustling of the silken purple curtains that the angels raise.
> Golden doors sculpted like those of the Florentine baptis-
> tery turn on their diamond hinges. The eye is swallowed
> up in splendid vistas; it embraces a succession of marvel-
> ous palaces through which glide beings of a superior na-
> ture. (ibid., p. 463)

After having yielded to the strong temptation of laughing
heartily at Balzac's incredible description of this musical moment, one should recognize its incongruity in the life of César
Birotteau. The transport that the author wishes to convey is like
the one reserved for the heroes of his "Études philosophiques."
Are the angels in the heaven of Louis Lambert the same ones
seen by César Birotteau? One must not mistake the probity of
Birotteau for a virtue, for although it may earn him a celestial
reward, it renders him impotent in his earthly struggle for
success. And when one investigates the highly comic tone of
Birotteau's musical communion with the heavenly spheres, one
begins to question the authenticity of his glorification. The
high-blown rhetoric merely echoes the tone initiated in the
novel's title, and the hyperbolic amplitude of both these elements are related to the character's smallness. When the reader

remembers the significance of the perfumer's failure in the light of his purposely inappropriate moments of glory, the hero emerges more abject than ever. "The business people who met the employee found there no vestige of the perfumer. The indifferent ones perceived an immense idea of human downfall in the aspect of this man upon whose face the blackest sorrow had put its mourning, who seemed ruined by what had never appeared in him: thought!" (ibid., p. 568) It is the absence of thought throughout the remainder of the novel that seals his fate and sets up the bitter comedy of his incongruence with life.

Thought comes too late to César Birotteau. It never comes at all to his brother or the equally unfortunate Paul de Manerville. Like the Birotteaus, Paul finds an adversary supremely gifted in the art of thinking. The revenge wrecked by Madame Evangélista is as cold-blooded and complete as that accomplished by Du Tillet and Abbé Troubert. The similarity among the three novels does not end until one considers the manner in which Paul brings about his own defeat and the comic terms in which this defeat is couched. Through blind stupidity, he baits the wrath of Madame Evangélista, thus preparing his doom as surely as his ingenuous brothers prepare theirs.

Upon his return to Bordeaux, Paul falls in love with Natalie Evangélista. She and her mother, living in genteel penury, hinge all their hopes upon this very advantageous match. The signing of the marriage contract is the central scene in the novel and the first of two moments that call forth full exploitation of comic hyperbole. The encounter is charged with intelligence. Madame Evangélista finds a brilliant foe in Paul's notary, the wily Mathias. In an elaborate series of bargains and discussions, Paul's future mother-in-law is forced to accept a marriage contract that ostensibly protects the de Manerville fortune. The young man's ignorance is the comic counterpoint to the shrewd manipulations over his fate. Paul does not even have the sense to listen to the proceedings. "In order to understand the scene, it is necessary to say that Paul and Natalie remained seated beside the fire, on a settee, and did not listen to a single article of the guardian's reckoning" (*Le Contrat de mariage, 3*, 149). Paul and Natalie flirt and hold hands, blissfully unaware of the serious dealings that are to decide their future. As Madame Evangélista realizes that she is about to lose this preliminary battle, Balzac's technique of dramatic contrast is manifested.

> The moment of silence that these four characters then observed is impossible to describe. Master Mathias, like a victor, waited for the signature of the two people who had believed they could despoil his client. Natalie, unable to comprehend that she was losing half of her fortune, Paul, ignorant of the fact that the house of Manerville was winning it, still laughed and chatted. Solonet and Madame Evangélista looked at each other, the former containing his indifference, the latter a throng of irritated feelings. (ibid., p. 151)

This silent confrontation of foes appeals to Balzac. He stops the action to focus upon the incongruence of the scene, and the focus he chooses is the comic ignorance of Paul. One has no right to such ignorance; the hero will pay for it dearly. Madame Evangélista never forgives him and goads her daughter into ruining Paul financially and making his life a misery.

The second important example of comic hyperbole occurs in the final pages of the novel and is used to reveal the extent of Paul's blindness. Before sailing to India in an attempt to remake his fortune, he receives a patently insincere letter from Natalie. In it she announces her pregnancy. Paul, totally infected by stupidity and ingenuousness, fails to realize that, due to certain constants in Mother Nature's timetable, the baby cannot be his. Then he reads a letter from his friend Henri de Marsay, in which the duplicity of Natalie and her mother is bluntly exposed. His reaction is outrageously funny in its inappropriateness.

> "What did I ever do to them?" he asked himself. This is the question of silly men, of weak men who, seeing nothing, are unable to foresee. He cried out, "Henri! Henri!" to his faithful friend. Many men would have gone mad. Paul went to bed. He slept that profound sleep which follows huge disasters, and which seized Napoleon after the battle of Waterloo. (ibid., p. 206)

The ingenuous man is always spared the terrible agony of complete realization. Blind and unwise in action, he falls dazedly to defeat, capable only of an instinctive cry. At the moment when all the hidden springs that have been governing his life are finally revealed, when literally no effort is needed to comprehend once elusive reasons, causes, and motives, the stupid man is still shackled by his infirmity. César Birotteau mumbles a prayer; his brother stares vacantly into space; Paul de Manerville cries out weakly and then falls fast asleep. The impossible musical transport of the perfume salesman is analogous to the coupling of Paul and Napoleon. The ludicrous disproportion implied in the comparison merely serves to portray the epic dimensions of Paul's insensitivity. These men, victims of their ingenuousness, are not permitted a moment of true lucidity; it would be contrary to their character. In the order of the Balzacian universe, they are not tragic heroes. Denied that moment of high tragedy when the hero must stare at the total reality of his fate, the ingenuous failures in *La Comédie humaine* emerge as truly unenlightened victims. The very key to their victimization is exactly this unenlightenment.

CHAPTER 3

The Passionate: The Irony of Degradation

Passion is a source of energy and permits its channeling and concentration. The most notorious successes in *La Comédie humaine,* Du Tillet, Troubert, and of course Vautrin, are intensely passionate men, offering up the whole of their beings to the satisfaction of a lust for power. They seek to dominate, to impose themselves, to exercise their will, to act. The passion that is an ingredient in their success is one that is directed toward reality and plunges the individual into an especially intimate relationship with the material circumstances of his moment in time. This proximity allows for the absolute awareness displayed by a character such as Vautrin, whose success is a foregone conclusion.

There are characters, however, whose passions do not direct them toward reality, who are, through their excessive desires, rendered incapable of functioning properly in the world at large. Such desires are focused instead upon other human beings in a relationship traditionally called love but more precisely described as the surrendering of one's humanity to another. The consuming passion that motivates the great loves in *La Comédie humaine* is exclusive, blinding, single-minded. In its total attachment to the object loved, it leaves the lover without sufficient force or will to enter into life's struggle. Since he is unaware of reality, the passionately obsessed is especially vulnerable to the naturally destructive elements that are always at play in the world.

It is the very quality of passion which furnishes the author with the dominant imagery and paradoxical directions he uses in describing these catastrophes of love. Irony is the device that appears most frequently, and it stems from passion's capacity to uplift as well as degrade. The postures of characters like Goriot and Baron Hulot appear even baser when seen in relation to the nobility of Madame de Beauséant and Adeline Hulot. Love offers two possibilities and two different levels of failure. One is selfless and ennobling, the other selfish and vilifying. Love is always destructive, and yet the author never forgets that it is a proof of humanity and therefore praiseworthy. While men's worth is measured by love, another face of love renders men worthless. This paradox controls Balzac's attitude. The failures of Hulot and Goriot emerge as simultaneous acts of treason to their humanity and affirmations of this same humanity. Therein lies the irony pregnant in each degrading situation to which they are submitted. The animal imagery used to portray their dehumanization artistically reinforces this conceptual paradox.

Le Père Goriot, which is in some ways the most explicit and concise artistic expression of Balzac's sociological thesis, offers us an excellent framework within which to judge the effects of destructive passion. A panorama encompassing many aspects of society as seen through the eyes of a central character, the novel is organized like a lesson. Rastignac is the schoolboy, and life the curriculum. The reader, along with this character, learns that true, blinding love is a decided liability in the real world. Rastignac, at the novel's end, can defy Paris with confidence. Sobered of his illusions, he begins his attack on life, firm in the conviction that he will not make the elementary errors committed by the failures who appear in the novel. With a mentor like Vautrin and the graphic examples of Goriot and

Madame de Beauséant before his eyes, Rastignac extracts meaning from the lesson.

Perhaps the most accurate appraisal of Goriot and of his passion is made by the Duchess of Langeais, as she recounts the old man's story to Rastignac. The Duchess, whose ill-fated love life is described in the novel bearing her name, is herself destroyed by passion. Her observations on one of love's victims are therefore particularly interesting. They bear a great measure of personal conviction, a sympathy reinforced by her own experience.

> Our heart is a treasure; empty it all at once and you are ruined. We no more forgive a sentiment for revealing itself completely than we do a man who has not a penny to his name. This father had given everything. For twenty years he had given his entrails, his love; he had given his fortune in one day. The lemon well squeezed, his daughters left the rind on the street corner. (*Le Père Goriot*, 2, 911)

The Duchess of Langeais perceives that the lover is doomed when the object of his affection does not reciprocate. As the self is irretrievably spent, the lover is inevitably dehumanized. The image of the squeezed lemon is especially well chosen, suggesting at once the bitterness of Goriot's lot and the nonhuman form he has assumed. The Duchess of Langeais describes the heart as a treasure, but she might describe it more accurately as a luxury. Goriot's initial mistake is allowing himself to be ruled by the dictates of his most urgent paternal instinct. By satisfying the every wish of his daughters, he jeopardizes his utility and puts a term to the role that he can play in their lives. Since his whole identity is contained in his fatherhood, when he can no longer fulfill the function of that position, he has destroyed himself. Having despoiled himself of all material advantage, Goriot is no longer useful to a system that is so completely oriented toward wealth. As the Duchess of Langeais states, the world simply does not pardon a poor man. Sentiment and

feeling are judged solely on a monetary standard. Love must
in some way be made tangible in the pragmatic Balzacian universe. Put in its most primitive terms, Goriot, when he has no
more money to give his daughters, can no longer love them
according to their needs. He has outlived his usefulness, thrown
away his fortune, the only arm he had for defense, and is left
with a single possession, his passion. The pressed lemon is a
brutally precise image of Goriot, denied his function in life,
emptied of his vitality.

Seen in this light, the old man's ravings, when Madame de
Restaud comes to ask him for money, take on a horrible kind of
logic. As we later learn during the deathbed scene, Goriot is
always aware of the truth. He realizes the nature and extent
of his importance to his daughters, and one can understand his
frustration when forced to miss the opportunity of affirming
his paternity. His beloved Nasie, from whose house he is ex-
cluded and whose visits to him have become increasingly rare,
asks him for money, help, these two materializations of his
affection. He offers to rob, to kill, to sell his own body, but then
admits the futility of such gestures.

> All right, I must die, all I can do is die. Yes, I am no longer
> good for anything. I am no longer a father, no! She asks,
> she needs, and I, wretch, I have nothing! Ah, you invested
> in annuities, old scoundrel, and you had daughters! But
> don't you love them? Die, die like the dog that you are!
> What, I am less than a dog, a dog would not act thus!
> (ibid., p. 1046)

Goriot sees his very humanity menaced by his inability to satisfy
the needs of Anastasie. Without money, his passion cannot
express itself. Since his whole life is consecrated to this passion,
he has lost his raison d'être. Truly, he is less than a dog.[1]

---

1. A systematic analysis of animal metaphor is made by L.-F. Hoffmann
in "Les Métaphores animales dans 'Le Père Goriot,'" *L'Année balzacienne*
(Paris, 1963), pp. 91–106.

The process of his dehumanization establishes one of the dominant tonalities in the novel. The example he sets for Rastignac is a vivid one, and it is characterized by willful self-destruction and the perversion of life. As we have seen in previous cases, Balzac expresses this both symbolically and explicitly. He is determined to present the ambiguity of Goriot's position in most unambiguous terms. He bends his whole rhetoric to the task of exposing the paradox of Goriot's ennobling self-degradation. This is a constant problem facing Balzac, a price he must pay for attempting to straddle the real and the ideal worlds. The images tend to emphasize Goriot's animality and distortion of life, while his nobility is suggested through implication and reflection.

The final condition of Goriot takes on stature through its inevitability. According to Goriot's definition of paternity, the better he fulfills the role, the quicker he will reach the end of his resources and therefore cease to be a father. This is a bitter irony. Having abdicated the other aspects of his personality, he has nothing upon which to rely, literally no other identity. He has lost all personality by striving for the ultimate expression of fatherhood. "He saw that his daughters were ashamed of him, that they loved their husbands, and that he would be detrimental to his sons-in-law. He had then to sacrifice himself. He sacrificed himself because he was a father; he committed an act of self-banishment" (ibid., p. 911). In his exaggerated desire to be the perfect father, he denies his existence and puts his paternity in fatal jeopardy. We are once again reminded of the contiguity of nobility and degradation.

The novel shows Goriot during his decline; the reader is permitted to examine the symptoms of his disease in their ugliest, most rotten phase. In a flashback, however, Balzac describes the changes that have occurred in Goriot's life, showing the gradual absorption of his personality into his passion. As is to be expected, the author carefully attaches the moral changes to very obvious physical ones, thus mirroring and magnifying the more subtle traits of personality in their easily discernible concretizations. With an ironic touch, the financial decline of Goriot's fortune is symbolized, inversely, by his inglorious rise in the Pension Vauquer. Beginning in a quite comfortable apartment on the building's first floor, he meets his fate in an incredibly miserable attic, barely furnished and virtually exposed to the elements. The author's ambivalence to Goriot is implicit in this position. Goriot's alienation from humanity is reflected in his eschewal of civilizing comforts. He discards the objects that represent men's mastery over their environment and differentiate them from animals. And yet, this literal rise in the pension puts him closer to heaven, the realm of ideals, where love has its only relevance. Thus, Balzac astutely presents contrary viewpoints in this single, versatile image, incidentally stressing Goriot's animality by an inference to his spirituality.

The changes in the hero's physical aspect, however, contain no germ of an increased spirituality. The flesh remains the flesh, and its corruption signals the physicality of passion. When Goriot first arrives at the Pension Vauquer, he is still an attractive man, one who has aged gracefully. With the loss of his fortune and separation from his daughters, he progressively crumbles into ruin. Physical discomfort and emotional chagrin take their toll, the years avenge themselves, and Goriot comes to truly merit the appellation *père*. "He became thinner and thinner; the calves of his legs grew flabby, his face, swollen by bourgeois happiness, became tremendously wrinkled; his forehead was creased, his jaw stood out. During his fourth year at Rue Neuve-Sainte-Geneviève, he no longer resembled himself" (ibid., p. 869). Nature refuses to tolerate this useless being, and Goriot is forced to pay a heavy price for the meager fruits of his passion. The self-indulgent illusions that protected him during the youth of his daughters cannot stand the shock of such total unhappiness. He is thus a pauper in two ways—a stranger to both the happy father and extremely comfortable bourgeois who had come to live at the Pension Vauquer, four years previously.

Balzac translates this surrender of life into the distortion of a nonhuman image. Goriot's abdication of self is voluntary and absolute, symbolized in the incident concerning his dead wife's luncheon service. One day, Madame Vauquer sees Goriot fondling a gilded plate and learns that it was the very first gift he had received from his wife. He treasures it as he does no other object in the world. Expressing himself with his habitual exaggeration, Goriot says: "You see, Madame, I would prefer to scratch the earth with my nails than to part with this" (ibid., pp. 861–62). The connection between Goriot and the plate serves two purposes. His visceral commitment functions as a premonition of his increasing animality, and the eventual sacrifice of the object shows the extent of his spiritual suicide, his dehumanization. In the sacrifice of his will, his common sense, he offers up his being on the altar of passion. The luncheon service is sold for his daughters. "He held fast to it as to his life" (ibid., p. 886). Disposing of the plates, which he had first pounded and bent out of shape, is the symbolic act which summarizes his life. His personality is warped, graceless, literally pounded out of shape, and he himself is destroyed by his passion. He is a failure as a human being. Since he virtually no longer exists, the act of giving away the precious luncheon service can be performed without compunction. Having already given away his life, the object most important to that life has lost its value.

Vautrin successfully analyzes the true character of Goriot, even though he mistakes paternal affection for an old man's romantic dalliance. In fact, the two are closely related. Vautrin, with his penetrating eye, his tremendous experience, and his unerring instinct for the truth, plumbs the depths of Goriot's soul. "People like that seize an idea and never let go. They are only thirsty for a certain water taken at a certain fountain, and it is often foul; to drink there, they would sell their wives, their

children, they would sell their soul to the devil" (ibid., p. 885).
The emphasis on instinct in the reference is not gratuitous. All
is passionately unleashed instinct with Goriot; reason and judgment no longer play roles in his existence. Every breathing moment is now consecrated to the frustrated love for his daughters.
Blinded to all proporation, alien to the system into which he was
born, his religion is paternity and his goddesses are Delphine
and Anastasie. Why should he hesitate to sell his soul for his
faith? Goriot is not loath to admit the fact that he has actually
sold his soul, if not to the devil, then to his daughters. "Actually
. . . what am I? A poor cadaver whose soul is wherever my
daughters are" (ibid., p. 945). Goriot has done high treason to
the human race. His previously discussed outburst of self-damnation, in which he esteems himself lower than a dog, takes on
grim significance when one considers it in relation to another
self-evaluation, made under less hysterical circumstances. Goriot
is determined to explain his personality to Rastignac and spares
no grizzly detail. One does not doubt for a moment the failure
of this man who passionately disposes of his humanity. "I love
the horses which draw them and I would like to be the little dog
that they hold on their laps" (ibid., p. 945). Goriot envies the
horses and dogs which are more important to Delphine and
Anastasie than their father. His failure as a human being is
illustrated no more graphically than in these few words. Balzac's
pity for Goriot is tempered by this character's epic disloyalty to
other men. The author, obsessed by the power of the human
will, by the transcendental nature of human beings, can feel
only intense loathing for this creature during such moments of
debasement.

Ruthlessly pursuing the seeds of this debasement Balzac uncovers the shocking truth that feeds Goriot's passion. He provides futher evidence of the character's degradation, attesting
to the shabbiness of his ungenuine paternity. Goriot at once
personifies fatherhood and is supremely unfit to be a father. He
is therefore unfaithful to the cause he most fervently serves,

further disqualifying himself from humanity. In his relationship to Delphine and Rastignac, gleefully sharing the secret of their romance and so anxious to live near his daughter's young lover, Goriot bears a striking resemblance to the typical maid of the typical *lorette*. In this case, the *lorette* is Rastignac, and the wealthy keeper is Delphine Nucingen, née Goriot. But an ulterior motive explains Goriot's wholehearted approbation of the Eugène-Delphine liaison. He wishes vicariously, and perhaps not so vicariously, to share in the sensuality of the young lovers. He craves physical proximity to his daughter and basks in the affection that reigns in the love nest that is Rastignac's apartment. If one can, for a moment, forget the image of the wronged, Learlike father, Goriot's actions emerge in all their luridness.

> The whole evening was spent in childishness, and old Goriot was not the least mad of the three. He lay down at his daughter's feet in order to kiss them; he looked for a long time into her eyes; he rubbed his head against her dress; finally he did all the foolish things that the youngest and tenderest lover would have done. (ibid., p. 1027)

With a heavy hand, Balzac describes the unusual fatherly passion of Goriot, which has deep roots in overt eroticism. Because of this, Goriot lies outside the pale of those particular values that function within the Balzacian universe. The father is no longer true to his role. His passion is pushed to such an extreme that it does not fit into the area prescribed by the rules of paternity. A father who makes mistresses out of his daughters has clearly lost sight of his role in society. He has consciously let his exaggerated passion lead him to his doom. "My daughters were my vice, they were my mistresses, in a word, they were everything!" (ibid., p. 1069) Goriot is unbecoming to his species; he falls into the oblivion reserved for all the incongruents of *La Comédie humaine*.

Goriot, however, is more than a crazed old man delighting
in the pleasure of seeing and touching his daughters. His sacrifice is one of those noble but vain gestures of defiance against
the pettiness of normal existence. Balzac has the profoundest
respect for the figure of the outcast and therefore assigns Goriot
to the same category designated for the noble Madame de
Beauséant. Rastignac, who has observed at close hand the
agonies of these two characters, comments on their similarity.
" 'Madame de Beauséant flees, this one dies,' he said. 'Beautiful
souls cannot remain for long in this world. How, in fact, can
great sentiments find a place in a society that is petty, small,
superficial' " (ibid., p. 1065). These creatures, so tortured by
their passions, are truly beautiful souls. They have nothing to
do with a world that excludes their sentiments, their sublime
gestures, their dedication.

  Madame de Beauséant is the sum of grace, beauty, generosity,
a product of all that the author considers best in the aristocracy.
In spite of these traits, or perhaps because of them, she is
destroyed by the same vulnerability that spells the failure of
Goriot. Wearing her heart on her sleeve, she neglects to hide
her love for the dandy Ajuda-Pinto from a very curious Parisian
society. Her first mistake, however, is to permit herself a genuine
love in a world where love must eventually bow to money.
She misjudges her possibilities for happiness, thus leaving herself open to the hard gaze of a ruthless world. Giving a ball
on the very night she learns of Ajuda-Pinto's intention to marry
the wealthy Mademoiselle de Rochefide, she must bare her
grief to her guests, undergoing a kind of public failure. She,
like Goriot, is offered up by society as a propitiatory sacrifice
to the voracious machine of existence.

  The most interesting aspect of the Goriot-Beauséant relationship is the way in which it illustrates the basic duality of
purpose that runs through *La Comédie humaine,* a duality that
incidentally controls the dramatic progression of *Le Père
Goriot.* Praise and damnation, failure and success are constantly

shifting polarities for the author, controlled by his shifting balance between the real and the ideal. Janus-like, he is often neutralized by the simultaneity with which he views the fact of past evidence and the ideal of future potential. Thus, he faces an unalterable paradox in his feelings about Goriot, the "Christ of Paternity" who yearns for his daughters' caresses as he lies in their laps like a dog. The major burden of suggesting the old man's capacity for beatification, spiritual success, sublimation through love, falls upon Madame de Beauséant. We are confronted with the author's irresistible attraction to the mirror of character reflection, which so clearly reveals his philosophical ambivalence and his literary obsession with antithesis. Madame de Beauséant suffers in noble silence, fully cognizant of the risk she runs in submitting to sincere love and ready to accept her harsh failure. At the ball, she pridefully exhibits her life, somehow knowing that the cause of her sacrifice, her glowing human sincerity, is infinitely more important than her defeat. Goriot, a victim of the underside of passion, expires on a filthy bed, in a paroxysm of madness atrociously compounded by lucidity. The apotheosis of Madame de Beauséant is an exultant mixture of courage and resignation.

> "Let's go downstairs. I do not want them to think that I am crying. I have eternity before me, I will be alone, and no one will ask me to account for my tears. Yet another glance at this room." She stopped. Then, after having hidden her eyes for a moment with her hand, she dried them, bathed them with clear water and took the student's arm. "Onward," she said. (ibid., p. 1061)

Madame de Beauséant has a superabundance of nobility, enough so that she can lend some to miserable old Goriot, her brother in passion. Her ability to transfigure worldly failure casts an uplifting light upon her fellow martyr, thereby mitigating the animality and degradation that, by contrast, her noble presence has imposed upon him.

Madame de Beauséant and Goriot define Rastignac's world with a set of contiguous, and in some ways identical, extremes. This unity within diversity is the kind of device that appeals to Balzac, enabling him to suggest the paradoxes of existence within a single literary framework and to remain consistent to an established tonality. Thus, he can posit the crisis of Rastignac's life in terms of two characters who are dear to the young man, who resemble each other, and who represent two kinds of failure in the eyes of the world. Madame de Beauséant, through her spiritualization, and Goriot, through his degradation, prove to Rastignac the uselessness of passion, the self-destructive effects of sincere love. He sees before his eyes a saint and a subhuman creature. In the last pages of the novel he is shuttled from Goriot's bedside, to the ball of Madame de Beauséant, and then back again to witness the old man's death agony. Life is explained to him spatially and conceptually, and his final choice is described in the same way. Rastignac, standing on the highest point of the cemetery, Père-Lachaise, sheds his final tear, buries his sincerity with Goriot, dies to the world of the passionate, and challenges Paris with what must be a premonition of success. Set on the path by the omniscient Vautrin, led to this place of death by the saint and the groveling dog, he leaves behind his heart and is ready to face the world on its own terms.

In the progression of *La Comédie humaine*, *Le Père Goriot* and the Vautrin–de Rubempré series of novels stand as the most complete expressions of the author's universe. In these works, the full canvas of society is analyzed, and the author's rhetoric displays its most brilliant versatility. It is in *La Cousine Bette*, however, that life's truths are viewed in their most atrocious form. It is as if Balzac had gazed too long and too deeply into the seething mass of existence. *La Comédie humaine* remains incomplete in the author's masterplan, but one wonders if the unwritten works could have gone beyond the horror of

La Cousine Bette. In this novel, riddled with infection and crumbling with decay, all that is human is thoroughly debased. The failure is that of existence at large. Men have ceased to be men, have surrendered to the basest face of their nature, and through a dreadful intimacy, have contaminated each other with the disease of unchecked passion. It is a process of mutual degradation, where the once human being sinks to his lowest state in *La Comédie humaine.*

Bette herself stands at the center of this spider's web, imposing her animal-demonic presence upon the other characters and then feeding on their corruption. She and Valérie Marneffe, the double we have come to expect of Balzac, literally devour the world. Bette learns from the beautiful Valérie about Wenceslas' infidelity; this sets off the chain reaction that eventually destroys all the major characters in the novel. The sheer animal force of her hatred gives a clear portent of her destructive potentiality.

> The face of the woman from Lorraine had become terrible. Her black and penetrating eyes had the fixity of a tiger's. Her face resembled that which we attribute to a pythoness, she clenched her teeth to prevent them from chattering, and a frightful convulsion made her limbs tremble. She slipped her deft hand between her hat and her hair in order to seize the latter and hold up her head which had become too heavy; she burned! The smoke of the fire which ravaged her seemed to pass through her wrinkles as through so many crevasses furrowed by a volcanic eruption. It was a sublime spectacle. (*La Cousine Bette, 6,* 223–24)

The power of nature is sublime but terrible. All that is human in Bette is eradicated in this eruption of passion. She is thrown out of herself, remade by forces consonant with primitive nature and opposed to the intelligence and spirituality that define men. Her potency is irresistible, especially when abetted by the luxurious malevolence of Valérie Marneffe. Bette's masculinity, suggested by her relationship with Wenceslas, is seconded by the eternal mistress, the ubiquitous prostitute Valérie. The wedding of animal passion, masculine force, and feminine seductiveness is invincible. The world's limits conspire to auto-destruction.

Balzac is not satisfied with the explicit intention in pairing Bette and Valérie. Constantly searching to thicken the fictional world, he creates Marneffe, Valérie's husband, a deputy from the land of the dead, who comes to putrefy the living. This character, in his very inactivity, looms as the most constant symbol of the novel's decay. While Bette and Valérie are driving, destructive forces, Marneffe is the well from which they draw their evil, a quasi-living reminder of that which they will become.

> Destroyed by those debaucheries particular to great capi-
> tals and described by the Roman poets (for which our
> modern prudery has no name), Marneffe had become
> hideous, like a wax anatomy model. However this walking
> disease, dressed in beautiful cloth, balanced his skinny
> legs in elegant trousers. This dried out chest was scented
> with white linen; musk extinguished the fetid odors of
> human decay. (ibid., p. 271)

Marneffe is the master pimp, the unspeakable pervert. His life is consecrated to passion, and his punishment, with Dantesque irony, renders him unfit for passion. Compounding the irony with a swath of rich cloth, the author portrays a self-indulgent, elegant society dancing to its death on rotten legs. Marneffe plays the sweet music, Valérie and Bette lead the grand march, and Hulot and Crevel follow in obedient tow.

The horrible death allotted to Valérie and her new husband, Crevel, at the end of the novel is an extension of the creeping disease prefigured by Marneffe. Valérie succeeds in destroying Hulot but destroys herself at the same time. Passion is at once her weapon and her downfall. Instead of abstracting herself and thus achieving a Vautrin-like immunity, she becomes a victim of passion, falls in love with the mysterious Brazilian, Henri Montès, incurs his vindictive jealousy, and is poisoned. Balzac fits this poison into the image framework of the novel. From the authoritative mouth of La Comédie humaine's family doctor, Bianchon (who was, incidentally, attendant upon the death of Goriot), comes this description:

> The poor creature who was once pretty, they say, is well punished for her sin, for today she is of an unspeakable ugliness . . . her teeth and her hair are falling out, she is like a leper, she horrifies even herself; her hands, frightening to see, are swollen and covered with greenish pimples; as she scratches herself, her nails fall out and remain in the wounds; finally all her extremities are being destroyed by the pus which is gnawing at them. (ibid., p. 503)

The author relishes the rhetoric of the horrible, having manufactured a mysterious infection that comes from the far-off jungles of the Amazon, with symptoms culled from the yet more distant recesses of his morbid imagination. Balzac's Amazon is that primitive place where the forces of the great machine are present in their purest form, and it is only right that it should be the source of his world-killing malady.

But it is the novel's central character, Baron Hulot, who most fully traces the course of the passionate failure. The forces emitted by Bette and Valérie and the shadow cast by Marneffe eventually converge upon this disintegrating man. His journey through life is a sloughing off of humanity just as complete as that of Goriot, and perhaps more so. Goriot partakes in the redemption of Madame de Beauséant, his heavenly intercessor, while Hulot betrays his Beatrice.

The novel recounts two journeys: Hulot and his wife, Adeline, take leave of each other and travel to the poles of existence.

As she becomes more ethereal, sublimated by an ideal of con-
jugal devotion, he withers away, consumed by passion. As in
the case of Goriot, the change in Hulot is described in terms
of an accelerated aging. There is, however, one important difference between the father and the lover. Goriot's aging is
basically involuntary, while Hulot, out of a pathetic submission
to his passion, consciously ages himself. He blindly succumbs to
flattery designed for the aged. As Valérie tells him that "White
hair goes marvellously with your face" (ibid., p. 270), the echo
of Frosine's cosmetic advice to Harpagon resounds in its sono-
rous falsity.[2] Hulot falls prey to the flattery, takes off his
corset, stops dyeing his hair, and removes all vestige of youth
from his appearance. This only signals an inner aging. Each
of his perfidies brings him closer to becoming the derelict
whom Madame Hulot rescues from a Parisian slum, near the
end of the novel. Each time he betrays his wife, her sacrifice
becomes that much more noble, and he becomes that much
more inhuman. "An old man, who seemed eighty, his hair
entirely white, his nose reddened by the cold in a face pale
and wrinkled like that of an old woman, walked with a drag-
ging step" (ibid., p. 465). Hulot is no longer himself. The
metamorphosis reserved for all of passion's victims is his inevitable end.

Yet this novel is not truly the story of the failure of the passionate. That story has been told many times previously in
La Comédie humaine. The curve of failure so obvious in novels
like *Illusions perdues* and *César Birotteau* is distorted in *La
Cousine Bette.* The point from which the characters begin is
already so low that they can only sink deeper into the slime
in which they are already swimming. Having dehumanized
them at the novel's outset, the author indulges in a development
of the rhetoric of their degradation. The destruction of Hulot,
Crevel, Valérie, and Bette is the last gasp from a body prac-

2. Molière, *L'Avare,* II.5.

tically dead. Somehow, in the novel's final pages, Hulot's failure loses importance, and he is resuscitated to participate in the most resounding failure of all, one that is irrefutable proof of corruption's power. Balzac's heaven is infected by it. Adeline Hulot, a model of wifely devotion, a sister to the host of *anges* that fills the pages of *La Comédie humaine*, symbolically admits the weakness of virtue. This occurs after her death, caused by overhearing her unrepentant husband promise marriage to a servant girl. "And one saw this rare occurence: tears coming out of the dead woman's eyes. The ferocity of Vice had conquered the patience of the angel, from whom, on the edge of Eternity, there escaped the only word of reproach that she had ever uttered in her entire life" (ibid., p. 524). Balzac lost the battle along with Adeline. Any illusions he might have professed about human perfectibility were false. Not even the angel could save Hulot. The heightened humanity, the beauty of life, mirrored in these tears wrought from dead eyes, represent the author's last anguish over the failure of the world's soul.

CHAPTER 4

The Weak: The Rhetoric of Character

The most thoroughly chronicled career in *La Comédie humaine* is that of Lucien de Rubempré.[1] Through almost all the seven novels grouped under the titles *Illusions perdues* and *Splendeurs et misères des courtisanes* this character assumes a wide assortment of shapes, undergoes countless transformations, and eventually succumbs under the weight of a life surfeited with failure. Everything that Lucien touches becomes tainted with his failure, a failure typically Balzacian and thus never capricious. It comes as the natural result of a given set of conditions. Lucien earns his successive failures, by making the mistakes that prove his undoing, mistakes stemming from an inability to cope with the rigors of existence. The rude lessons that life tries to teach him form a curriculum determined by a hard and ruthless world.

The very dimensions of Lucien's portrait impart to him a high measure of importance in Balzac's gallery of creations. In Lucien can be seen the versatility of the author's literary invention, the methods he uses in giving scope to the character and allowing him to illuminate the world he inhabits. The protagonist becomes a rhetorical device, at once varying the texture of the

1. Gaëton Picon, in his preface to *Illusions perdues,* Le Club du meilleur livre (Paris, 1958), comments upon the pivotal nature of the novels in which Lucien de Rubempré appears.

gargantuan novel sequence and holding together the various themes and milieus with his fundamental traits. Provincial life, Paris, and a whole range of societal situations come under the author's scrutiny and are given a frame in the person of Lucien de Rubempré. The frame constantly changes color and texture as it receives reflected light from the objects and individuals it contains. Lucien's weakness is overtly commented upon by others and is indirectly pointed up by their presence. This process of reflection and contrast is a cornerstone of Balzac's art and an organizing influence on his novels. Through it he manages to accomplish two important goals: render the protagonist credible by lengthening his stature in shadow and reflection and enclose the sprawling world of the novel within the identifiable locus of a single character. The most highly developed examples of this technique are *Illusions perdues* and *Splendeurs et misères des courtisanes.*

By studying the many stages in the career of Lucien de Rubempré, the fate of the weak man trying to make his way in the world can be traced as it appears in *La Comédie humaine.* This weak man is a figure that haunts Balzac. The author's fascination with the force of *volonté* is well known, and it is essential to remember the importance it holds in his imagination and the imprint it leaves on his novels. The will is a concrete force which, if focused and concentrated, is all-powerful. It permits one to exert superhuman strength and vision. The lack of such a will dooms men to failure. The world constructed by the author is a hard one, and only the very strongest can survive the rigors of its laws. Others succumb because they lack the fortitude, the ability to dominate, the perspicacity which the never-ending and ruthless struggle for survival demands from them. As the author repeatedly outlines the failure of the weak man, he solidifies his arguments concerning the validity of strength and will power. By referring to the laws that govern the Balzacian universe the reader can observe the weak man's gestures leading to failure and follow the course of the novel armed with this special knowledge. He is put into this all-seeing, all-knowing position to gain his credence. The career of Lucien de Rubempré is a painful exhibition of the inevitable failure of weakness.

The reader's first view of Lucien is a revealing one. Balzac is a firm believer in the rule of suitability, which decrees that each man has a place in the universe into which he fits more or less comfortably. His refusal or inability to fit into this niche will doom him. Lucien's brain orients him to one course, but his temperament makes him opt for another. "Although destined for the highest inquiries into the natural sciences, Lucien enthusiastically chose the path of literary glory" (*Illusions perdues, 4,* 482). While intelligence seems to lead him to the realm of science, Lucien does not have the physical or moral constitution necessary to meet its demands. Moreover, his beauty is guaranteed to nurture pride and make him unfit for the kind of self-effacement that the life of a scientist demands. All this is obvious from Balzac's initial portrait of the character, which is, as usual, a mine of information, offering clues to psychological as well as physical traits. The author firmly believes in their coincidence, and the novelistic value of such a linking is something he does not ignore. This attempt at a physical representation of the character's more subtle human qualities serves to anchor the ephemeral in the tangible. It is another means of definition seized upon by this author who seeks to define all existence; it is another ordering element in the teeming mass of lives found in Balzac's novels.[2] The reader is meant to use the

2. The mystery locked in reality has been one of the most consistently studied problems of Balzac scholarship. Ernst Curtius, in his justly famed *Balzac,* French trans. Henri Jourdan (Paris, 1933), explored this area with great profit and intuition. "An attempt to embrace the secret of life, decipher its mysterious hieroglyphics, penetrate the hidden causes of all phenomena, thus was revealed to us the meaning of existence in Balzac" (p. 163).

portrait as a key to the character's personality, as a way of identifying and differentiating. More important, Balzac intends that the reader extrapolate by filling in this portrait with all that is implicit in each eyebrow, each nose, each tilt of the head. He can dispense with endless commentary for he has convinced the reader of the pertinence of physicality. It is thus incumbent on the reader to interpret the portrait, to decipher all that Balzac implies.

> Lucien struck the gracious pose sculptors have lent to the Indian Bacchus. His face had the distinctive lines of ancient beauty: he had a Greek forehead and nose, the velvety whiteness of a woman, eyes so black that they were blue, eyes full of love, and whose whites rivaled in freshness those of a child. (ibid., p. 485)

In such a graceful pose, Lucien is vulnerable to being toppled over with the greatest of ease. Balzac injects a more than slightly jaded tone of languor and lassitude into this description. The exotic element is served by an Indian Bacchus, ancient beauty, and a Greek nose and forehead. These traits are obviously chosen to suggest both the ascetic and the dissipated. The insistence on Lucien's femininity is prolonged and will be reiterated. Infantile, feminine, graceful, Lucien's beauty is a strange admixture which prevents him from following a regular course of life. What kind of man is he? His physical traits reveal that he will be debilitated by the various forces at work within him. Fickleness and vanity prevent him from making the decisions and taking the steps that might strengthen his will and insulate him against the ever-present currents of competition and greed at work in the world be chooses to inhabit. Balzac continues to fill in a portrait of uneasy harmonies, good traits that contain the germs of the young man's doom. He is referred to as a girl in disguise, complete with a pair of feminine hips, and he is endowed with an intuition to go along with his other womanly trappings. Lucien's later development can be explained in light

of the caricatural femininity posited by the author. The side of
Lucien that is most obviously womanlike will curse his life.
This deformation of his masculinity helps to explain his need
to submit and his ability to abdicate his will through moral
and physical prostitution. Journalism succeeds in subverting his
literary talent to its vulgar ends, and his homosexual relationship with Vautrin, superbly understated by Balzac, reduces him
to a shadow-like existence. The lugubrious assortment of fates
that awaits Lucien is prefigured in this initial portrait, in
which Balzac presents a character so easily molded and re-
created that the permutations it goes through, in over a thousand
pages of text, are not in the least bit incredible. The rearrange-
ment of his features and the treason committed against his sex
prove that there is literally nothing that Lucien will not attempt,
but there is very little for which he is fit.

Balzac seizes the opportunity to put Lucien's character into
relief by placing it side by side with the strikingly contrasting
one of David Séchard. This is a device typical of Balzac, who is
forever unwilling to abandon his characters to a universe ignorant of their existence. In these novels, crisscrossed and weighted
with echoes and relationships, the contrast between Lucien and
David is a prime example of the author's effort to anchor the
character in the reader's imagination. In this case, it is the perfect symmetry of the opposition that is memorable. The author
states that if these two characters had exchanged either temperament or physique they might have succeeded. Lucien's failure
will be a subject for probing examination; David, treated more
briefly, will manage to garner only a succès d'estime, while
actually failing in the eyes of most men. Balzac's love of
paradox permits him to be content with the overly pat contrast
that is the relationship between Lucien and David. If the
author's lack of subtlety is hardly of great literary merit, his
purpose is a valid one in the context of La Comédie humaine,
because it serves to point up once again the connection between

physical type and personality. The wrecked careers of both Lucien and David appear as examples of what occurs when the fate that nature has ordained for the individual is defied. In presenting this pair of characters, the author gives the reader a firm basis from which to deduce an alternative outcome to the novel. Lucien needed only to follow David's destiny, and he probably would have been a successful scientist. This alternative, planted in the reader's mind, amplifies the novel's fictional reality by grafting onto it an extra-fictional dimension.

Balzac is not content to merely describe the relationship between Lucien and David or to underline its irony. He takes advantage of it in order to dramatize Lucien's weakness. The poet betrays his closest friend, the better part of himself, in his desire to conquer provincial society. It is the first of his compromises, and its very shallowness and waste underline Lucien's easy cowardice. He is ready to sacrifice his professional honor as a poet and degrade his idyllic friendship simply because he fears embarrassment in the salon of Madame de Bargeton. In this first part of the novel, Lucien is torn between the good influence of his friend, his sister, and his mother and the desire to launch his career, no matter what the cost. "Lucien was so constituted that he went from evil to good, from good to evil with equal facility" (ibid., p. 517). It is this capacity for unlimited variance that throws light upon Lucien's terrible weakness. He is ever-repentant, ever-sinning, ever-unresolved. His beauty and charm win temporary pardon for the mistakes he commits, but they cannot fill the void left by his lack of will. Balzac makes this ambivalence plain by having Lucien reject his mirror image, David, in favor of Madame de Bargeton.

Lucien has not yet failed, but Balzac has given a variety of signs indicating that he will in the future. The weakness caused by a certain combination of personality traits will be stimulated by the adoration he receives from both Madame de Bargeton and his family. Fattened on a diet of praise, the beautiful white lamb will be offered up for slaughter on the altar of a world that tempts its victims to destruction. Balzac does not give the reader a chance to mistake his intention, as he cautiously explains the curse of Lucien's beauty.

> He was so seductive, his manners were so winning, he expressed his impatience and his desires so graciously, that he always won his case before even having spoken. This fatal privilege dooms more young people than it saves. Accustomed to the attentions elicited by their lovely youthfulness, happy in the selfish protection that the world accords a being which it likes (as it gives alms to the beggar who awakens sentiment or emotions), many of these grown-up children enjoy this favor instead of exploiting it. (ibid., pp. 571–72)

The importance of this passage lies in its insistence upon the implicit ruthlessness of the world at large, so often represented as a force menacing the individual. This world is truly one of the major forces in *La Comédie humaine,* and Balzac often personalizes it by putting it in direct opposition to the protagonist. In this instance, Lucien is compared to a beggar, a foreshadowing of the posture he will assume with increasing frequency throughout the novel.

As Lucien embarks upon the first Parisian phase of his career, he cuts himself free from the tenuous roots that so poorly anchor him in the soft ground of true friendship and family affection. He leaves Angoulême before his sister's wedding to David, and he takes with him money precious to the Séchard household, thus committing his first great acts of treason and setting the tone for a life riddled with hypocrisy. Hypocrisy, however, does not doom Lucien. It is rather an inability to willfully dedicate himself to hypocrisy, to rid himself of the several good intentions that cling to him with persistence. The weakness that seizes the balms of self-pity and self-reproach in the aftermath of wrongdoing prevents Lucien from fully profiting from his fight for success. Before leaving his friend, on his way

to meet Madame de Bargeton, "Lucien experienced one of the
most intense emotions of his life, and he threw himself into
David's arms" (ibid., p. 593). This act of self-pity is an excellent
key to Lucien's character. He is simply too weak to commit
himself. The many sides of his personality pull in opposite
directions, and while Lucien's egotistical unscrupulousness usually dominates, his caricature of a conscience is eventually
paralyzing. He cannot take a truly confident step over the bodies
that lie across his path.

As soon as he arrives in Paris, Lucien suffers his first failure.
"It was not a judgment, but a denial of justice. A deathly cold
seized the poor poet when de Marsay stared at him through
his lorgnette; the Parisian celebrity let his lorgnette fall in
such an odd way that it seemed to Lucien as if it were the
guillotine's blade" (ibid., p. 624). Balzac imposes infinite meaning on the lorgnette of Henri de Marsay, and justly so in terms
of *La Comédie humaine*. There is no more fitting focus into the
true workings of society than the eye of the consummate
Parisian dandy, de Marsay. He is one of those rare beings who
have mastered reality and can therefore judge it with complete
exactitude. The author's love of juxtaposition and reflection
bestows special meaning on the lorgnette. Lucien first reveals
his inexperience by the overly starched look of his new clothes.
He does not know how to manipulate the symbols that identify
the class to which he aspires. Henri de Marsay, impeccably
dressed, a master of the social gesture, chooses to brutally ex-
ecute Lucien with a lorgnette, symbol of society's useless but
necessary affectations.

Literally cut off from the *beau monde* through circumstance
rather than volition, Lucien finds himself leading the ideal life
for a young poet, studying at the Bibliothèque Sainte-Geneviève,
meditating, writing. The qualities that make him unfit for such
a life are put into relief by his new friend, Daniel d'Arthez.
At Angoulême, David Séchard and Lucien's mother and sister

were the points of contrast used by the author to shed light upon the hero's character. In Paris, it is d'Arthez and his idealistic friends of the Cénacle who judge Lucien indirectly by their example and openly by their opinions. Balzac constantly projects his point of view upon the novels by this use of a contrasting destiny, a contradictory life.

> "One cannot be a great man cheaply," Daniel said to him in a gentle voice. "Genius waters its works with its tears. Talent is a moral creature who has, like all beings, a childhood subject to sickness. Society rejects incomplete talents just as Nature bears away weak or deformed creatures. He who wants to rise above men must prepare himself for a great struggle, must recoil before no difficulty. A great writer is a martyr who will not die, that is all." (ibid., p. 647)

The oracular tone of this tirade is the one that Balzac uses whenever he attempts to describe the way of the world. Nature destroys the imperfect beings who are unable to fit into her great design.

The same method is used in *La Cousine Bette* to describe the failure of Wenceslas Steinbock. This character betrays his artistic promise just as surely as Lucien fails to fulfill the potential of his literary talent. The resemblance between these two characters, whose gifts are small but genuine, is striking. The Polish miniaturist achieves a quick success; Lucien too hears the Parisian public sing his praises. Yet both the poet and the artist inevitably fail; their respective successes are pathetically short-lived. The very nature of their success reveals their weakness, a weakness described by Balzac in tangible, physical terms. "It was success, but as it comes in Paris, that is to say madly, success that crushes the people who do not have the shoulders and the back to carry it, which, incidentally, happens often" (*La Cousine Bette*, 6, 219). The meaning of this observation is obvious. One needs strength to cope with success, more strength in fact than one needs to attain it. This is another law at work in Balzac's universe, and it makes its jurisdiction felt even in artistic endeavors.

Steinbock is a skillful miniaturist, capable of fashioning beautiful objects when he fully applies himself to the task. Under the iron hand of Lisbeth Fischer, he reaches his full artistic potential. One must see in Balzac's indictment of Lucien and Wenceslas a proud defense of the artistic calling. He defiantly describes its rigors, and the weak-willed men who pose as artists incur his most terrible wrath. In portraying their failure he finds ample opportunity to present his own artistic efforts in a most flattering light.

> But to produce, but to give birth, but to laboriously raise the child, put it to bed each night full of milk, kiss it every morning with the inexhaustible heart of a mother, to lick it clean when it is dirty, to clothe it a hundred times in the most beautiful garments which it incessantly tears; but not be discouraged by the convulsions of this mad life and to make of it an animated masterpiece which speaks to all glances in sculpture, all intelligences in literature, all memories in painting, all hearts in music: that is Execution and its works. (ibid., p. 318)

Clothing this description of the artistic experience in the garb of basic life processes is not gratuitous. Life and art are closely wedded in *La Comédie humaine.* The symbolic mechanism of *La Peau de chagrin,* for example, is simply an artful representation of life. Conversely, art is explained in terms of living, is constantly related to the great forces of the world. The successful artist, like Balzac, wages a superhuman struggle with this art and with the world at large, and out of this struggle greatness is forged. Lucien de Rubempré and Wenceslas Steinbock are most emphatically not of such caliber. The creative tension that is essential to the life of the artist cannot be tempered by ease, by distraction, by contentment. Basking in the love of his wife, lulled into laziness by the excitement of his first success, Wenceslas relinquishes his artistic will, his creative courage. Like Lucien, he gives in to a facile life.

These weak-willed men share many common traits; not the least important of these is their incapacity for self-examination. The author sees them most clearly, and for him their fates are inevitable. The alert reader perceives this inevitability in the signs, contrasts, and other indirect means at Balzac's disposition. There are, however, less subtle explanations of a given character's behavior, at moments in which the author's omniscience is plainly voiced.

> "There is in you," Michel Chrestien said to him, "a diabolical spirit with which you will justify in your own eyes the things most contrary to our principles: instead of being a sophist of ideas, you will be a sophist of action." "Ah! I fear you are right," said d'Arthez. "Lucien, you will conduct inside yourself admirable discussions in which you will be great, and which will lead you to reprehensible actions. . . . You will never be in agreement with yourself." (*Illusions perdues,* p. 662)

Unwittingly, the friends of the Cénacle have hit upon the reason for Lucien's failure. Being a sophist does not damn him. It is his ability for self-delusion, for seeming great in his own eyes, for true ignorance, that spells the failure of Lucien's projects. He is fit to become a journalist, the calling most despised by these idealistic young men. Lucien prefers to fool himself into thinking that all his perfidy is honorable. He must take the easy way. " 'I admit that I am not as strong as you are,' he said while looking at them in his adorable fashion. 'I do not have the back and the shoulders to hold up Paris, to struggle with courage' " (ibid., p. 662). Balzac again reverts to the familiar physical images in order to suggest the kind of struggle to which a man must submit in his quest for success. Lucien is hampered not only by his physical but also by his moral weakness, his coquettish need to appear adorable.

No warning has sufficient intensity to convince Lucien of his folly. Balzac is not content in presenting the hero as deaf to the good advice of friends. He puts Lucien face to face with his own destiny. He lets him see Raoul Nathan, a man of letters whom he admires, forced to grovel before a critic.

> Lucien, who saw himself there in embryo, had admired Nathan's book. He revered the author like a god, and he was stupefied by so much cowardice in front of a critic whose name and importance were unknown to him. "Would I ever act in the same way? Must one then abdicate dignity?" he asked himself. "Put your hat back on, Nathan, you have written a beautiful book and the critic has only written an article." (ibid., p. 699)

Lucien is clever enough to ask himself these searching questions, to realize the dreadful truth illustrated by an author's debasement of self, to wonder if he would be capable of a similar ego betrayal. In spite of this, he lets himself be drawn into the world of journalism. Lucien has a chance to change his destiny at a variety of turning points in his life, but his refusal to take the right and hard path proves that weakness will irrevocably doom him. In the desire to satisfy the most insistent cravings of his egotism, Lucien tramples his ideals and his right to self-esteem. This is a striking bent to auto-destruction. In response to an egotistical need, he endangers his power to exercise this very egotism. With the image of Nathan before his eyes, Lucien wills upon himself the same fate.

Balzac permits Lucien one last moment of nostalgia for the ideals of his still recent past. He wistfully evokes David and his serious Parisian friends of the Latin Quarter. "In remembering the evenings at the Cénacle, a tear glistened in the eyes of the poet" (ibid., pp. 712–13). This phrase has a twofold meaning. Most obviously, the author tries to preserve some sympathy for Lucien by making the hero aware of the significance of his compromise. As long as Lucien realizes the worth of the existence he is about to abandon, he has not yet lost all vestige of sensitivity. Yet this very realization is the key to the deeper meaning of the scene. Lucien's awareness, his acceptance of a situation that he might avoid, and his passing feeling of remorse are additional vivid proofs of his weakness. Lucien does not choose his new role with the unalloyed eagerness of the ruthless profiteer, nor does he have the excuse of the profiteer's insensitivity. Temptations that could appeal only to the impressionable and the feeble are Lucien's undoing. He is ready to barter his life and soul for the fugitive glory of the journalistic world.

Lucien's entrance into journalism gives Balzac the chance to vent his most bitter feelings against that profession. He sees it as an example of all that ails society at large. Ever alert for new ways to seize the world, to synthesize its rhythms and conflicts, Balzac projects onto the arena circumscribed by journalism the variety of experiences that Lucien encounters. The author benefits from the added intensity found in the back-biting, ruthlessly competitive journalistic milieu. By its very nature, it destroys that which is best in human nature. The intelligent man, this time Claude Vignon the critic, arrives upon the scene to describe the process.

> Over there, next to Coralie, there is a young man . . . what is his name? Lucien! He is handsome, he is a poet, and, what is more important, a clever man; ah well, he will enter one of those places of intellectual prostitution called newspapers. There he will waste his most beautiful ideas, he will dry out his brain, he will corrupt his soul, he will commit those anonymous acts of cowardice which, in the war of ideas, replace the strategy, pillage, arson, and

betrayal of the warfare of *condottieri*. And when, like
thousands of others, he has squandered his genius in the
service of speculators, those dealers in poison will leave
him to die of hunger if he is thirsty, and of thirst if he is
hungry. (ibid., pp. 739–40)

Lucien surrenders himself to journalism, a career that stimulates
his taste for ease, luxury, brilliance, and power. A weak man,
he can challenge only that which requires but a day or an hour
to be conquered. Strong men, like d'Arthez or David Séchard,
reply to challenges with the weapons of truth and wisdom;
Lucien's arms are those of facile wit. He succumbs to the dizzy
view from the height to which he momentarily soars, and while
he imagines that he will continue ever upward, he willfully
dives headlong into an abyss. The force he believes at his dis-
posal is not sufficient in a world that cannot in truth be van-
quished. The system created by journalism is faithfully described
by Claude Vignon. It feeds on its own talent with an eternal
voraciousness, and Lucien is helpless to its siren song.

Perhaps the most original aspect of the author's depiction of
weakness is his characterization of the journalistic profession
itself. His description remains fairly constant throughout *La
Comédie humaine*. He unmistakably wishes to condition the
reader into equating journalism with weakness and hypocrisy.
After Lucien's initial act of acceptance of the foul rules that
govern the new game he is about to play, no cause is too sacred,
no ideal too absolute to escape the casuistry of his pen. Lousteau
admirably characterizes the game. "My friend, a journalist is
an acrobat. You must get used to the hazards of the profession"
(ibid., p. 774). The reference to the acrobat suggests trickery,
deformation, and falsehood.

Lucien is not so ingenuous as to miss the point of Lousteau's
lesson, and yet the once idealistic poet from Angoulême accepts
the arms of hypocrisy without much protest. He devours them
in his weakness, the same weakness that allows him to justify

his new compromises. "Lucien was astonished listening to Lousteau; the journalist's words caused the scales to fall from his eyes, and he discovered literary truths that he had never even suspected. 'What you say,' he cried, 'is full of truth and commonsense'" (ibid., p. 776). Balzac's flair for comedy is obvious in this scene, and through it he dramatizes Lucien's weakness. The former idealist naïvely accepts Lousteau's version of the truth. His about-face has burlesque rapidity. The reader, who has before his eyes the author's depiction of reality, is shocked into the comic viewpoint by the incongruence of the situation.

The same qualities that attract Lucien to his new career had previously exercised their fascination over Etienne Lousteau. The weakness and hypocrisy of these two characters are the same. Lousteau, who remains in the background of *Illusions perdues,* is the object of considerably more attention in *La Muse du département.* This is still another study of the weak man's failure, and journalism is again used as its frame.

As in the case of Lucien, the faults of Lousteau are magnified by the virtues of other characters. Lousteau's spinelessness is seen in contrast with the strength of an exceptional woman, Dinah Piédefer, who, in spite of her determination and brilliance, sacrifices position and self-respect to the fiction of the journalist's love. Dinah is more than a match for Lousteau. She quickly analyzes the roots of his perpetual failures and of his refusal to leave the precarious position of newspaper critic. "She guessed why Lousteau had not conquered misery: he was lazy and lacked will" (*La Muse du département,* 4, 204). This lack of will, which the reader can readily appreciate, does not render Lousteau unfit for his role of critic. In fact the ease with which he handles a destructive pen is another proof of his weakness. He shares with Lucien a lack of convictions and an inability to commit himself, traits common to members of the newspaper profession as conceived by Balzac. "Addiction to the cigar conditioned the laziness of Lousteau. If tobacco dulls grief, it infallibly benumbs energy. Everything that the cigar snuffed out in his physical being, criticism annihilated in the morality of this fellow so easily attracted to pleasure" (ibid., p. 177). Balzac, with his gift for swift characterization, conjures up a vivid portrait of the hero in wisps of cigar smoke. We see the languid, graceful Lousteau, charming and pointless. The identifiable aroma of the cigar makes his weakness physical and sensory. The laziness suggested by the smoke is the exact antithesis of the kind of quality that Lousteau should possess for his life's struggle, and thus it is no surprise that he is doomed to failure. Through its illusoriness, Balzac incidentally comments on criticism, opposing it, by implication, to the solidity of his fiction.

The lack of will and penchant for laziness do not impede Lousteau from practicing the brand of criticism that is rampant in Paris. Such criticism, however, with its rash of hypocrisy, mendacity, and compromise, offers no chance of success to its exponents; it stimulates only their weakness. Lousteau and his weak cohorts put into sharp relief the one praiseworthy critic in *La Comédie humaine*. Claude Vignon, a character who never emerges from the periphery of Balzac's fiction, does make his presence felt as a partisan of honest criticism. Dinah Piédefer understands the difference between Lousteau and Vignon.

> The distance which separates Trade from Art was that which separated Claude Vignon from Lousteau. Dinah, whose perception was quickly sharpened, and whose intelligence had scope, had soon judged the literary attributes of her idol. She saw Lousteau working at the last moment, under the most dishonoring conditions, and *letting it go,* as painters say of a work in which *know-how* is lacking. (ibid., pp. 178–79)

The intellectual honesty of Vignon and the perspicacity of Dinah are standards that constantly loom up before the reader's eyes, standards against which Lousteau must be measured. His vindictiveness, facile wit, and flabby will are characteristics that tie him inextricably to Lucien. They make the same mistakes, and as Lousteau flaunts the illegitimacy of his child in the senseless gesture of mockery that is the birth announcement, one is forced to recall Lucien's silly, self-destructive attack on Madame de Bargeton and Baron de Châtelet. Relying upon this literary memory, the author establishes another bit of precedence to fill out the fictional lives he documents. But the ever-cautious Balzac does not fully trust his audience, and he provides an additional reference for judging Lousteau's petty vengeance. Raoul Nathan, another member of the shady newspaper-literary world to which Lousteau belongs, cannily appraises the impetuous defiance of the recent father. Balzac conveniently forgets the failure-ridden Nathan he condemns in *Une Fille d'Eve;* here, as he voraciously seizes upon Lousteau's blunder, Nathan is thoroughly aware of the strength that must be exerted in the arena of life. "This note proves that Lousteau lacks courage, good taste, dignity, that he knows neither the world nor public morality, that he insults himself when he does not know who else to insult. . . . this, sir, is a document that belongs in the archives of our time" (ibid., p. 180). It comes as no surprise that Lousteau remains a failure, unable to solidify his shaky position in the world of journalism, unable to find another outlet for his feeble talents and his pathetically small reservoir of will power. At the end of the novel he comes to beg money from Dinah, now reunited with her husband and restored to her rightful position in society. The journalist puts on his finest clothes, summons his most prideful manner, and capitalizes on his former mistress' lingering affection. Dinah complies, just as during their liaison she had provided him with the fortitude he lacked. But Lousteau fails to disguise himself from the reader. In the Balzacian universe, the man who succeeds never needs to beg.

Balzac uses the framework of love to define Lousteau's total

lack of will. Having come to Dinah with the intention of
utilizing affection as the lever for extortion, he is put into
vivid contrast with this noble woman, a woman in the mold
of Madame de Beauséant, capable of sacrificing all for love in
a final show of strength. The author is not unaware of the effect
created by the reversing of traditional sexual roles, bestowing
qualities of strength upon the woman and weakness upon the
man. It is a device he most tellingly exploits in *La Cousine Bette,*
dramatizing the relationship between Bette and Wenceslas. In
La Muse du département it is simply one in the series of signals
used to locate the personality of Etienne Lousteau.

The touchstone of any activity in *La Comédie humaine* is
volonté. The author's evaluation of the state of a character's
volonté is intended as an index in charting the novel's direction.
Lucien's moral untidiness and his uneasy fence-straddling inevitably sap his poor resources of *volonté.* "Thus, the spring of
his will, ceaselessly weakened by a laziness which made him
indifferent to the fine resolutions taken on those occasions when
he perceived his position in its true light, became totally ineffec-
tive, and soon responded no more to the strongest pressures of
misery" (*Illusions perdues, 4,* 822). Dissipation having consumed his precious energy, Lucien is easy game for cleverer and
stronger enemies who masquerade as his friends. His weakness
allows the clouding of his wit, the numbing of his judgment.
Lucien simply cannot observe the reality of his moment and is
thus incapable of acting in relation to its needs.

It is precisely at this apex, surrounded by supposed friends
and acclaimed as the most talented young critic in Paris, that
Lucien is undone. The Royalists, angered by caricatures of
Madame de Bargeton and Baron de Châtelet, hatch a conspiracy
designed for his ruin. Having learned that Lucien once craved
to assume his mother's noble name, de Rubempré, they try to
tempt him into their camp with promises of legitimatization.
Received by Madame d'Espard, taken into friendship by

Rastignac and the Duke de Rhétoré, Lucien walks blindly into the trap. But he does not abandon his journalist friends or his mistress. He is ever-willing to flit from side to side, seeking to please everyone while actually betraying all, himself in particular. Unable to muster enough will power to cast his lot with one party, he tries to satisfy both and destroys himself in the process. Balzac describes this weak young man running wildly from the aristocratic salons of Paris to the orgies of the journalists, stopping on the way to lose at the gaming tables. Any vitality he might have possessed is thoroughly neutralized by the polarity of his allegiances. Balzac uses his familiar device of extreme contrast to throw light upon his hero's shortcomings, thereby making the relationships and the artistic tensions readily apparent to the widest possible audience. Lucien, a pawn at home in neither camp, is the point of departure from which the author comments on basic social antagonisms. But more important to the art of the novel, these social antagonisms facilitate the pinpointing of Lucien's weakness. They dramatize his spineless ambivalence and schematize the rhythm of his degradation.

Events begin to turn against the idyllic couple, Lucien and Coralie. The money, once so conveniently furnished by Camusot, the actress' protector, is no longer forthcoming. Somehow, the first sign of misery, the first deprivation, brings on a host of others, and the financial situation of the poet and the actress becomes desperate. Lucien, neglecting to assure himself some security while leading the life of a rich young man, prepares his own fate. He has donned an expensive mask but does not have the means that will allow him to wear it for an extended period of time.

Lucien finds himself in an extremely vulnerable position. His financial future depends upon the vagaries of the publishing business, on the malicious editor, Dauriat, and on the shaky career of Coralie. By anchoring Lucien's chance for success in

a series of improbabilities Balzac indirectly comments upon the
hero's judgment and prepares the reader for the outcome.
Given Lucien's personality, these situations will prove to be
insurmountable. The frequency with which he must change
countenance, the number of conflicting interests he must serve
simultaneously, all these fragmentations of his will succeed in
pulverizing his *volonté*. Again capitalizing upon Lucien's former literary pretensions and reiterating the theme of self-
treason, Balzac shows him selling his soul to the highest bidder.
He relinquishes his novel, *L'Archer de Charles IX,* to populariz-
ing editors who desecrate the text in order to adapt it to the
most current and vulgar tastes of the public. The small sum he
realizes from this transaction disappears at the casino of Palais-
Royal. Lucien loses another bit of his soul in a game of chance.

The reader knows that the "higher order of logic" to which
Lucien so grandly refers is nothing more than his own egotistical
scramble for success. If he could totally dedicate himself to this
program he might have a chance for success, but weak Lucien
is a victim of serious second thoughts. "Lucien remained pensive
and sad for a few moments" (ibid., p. 844). The hesitation of

Balzac cannot resist the temptation of once again forcing
Lucien to listen to the voice of conscience, personified by his
idealistic friends of the Cénacle. They try to discourage him
from writing for a Royalist review, for in doing so he would
betray his liberal journalist friends. Lucien answers: "The reasons that make me act are drawn from a higher order of logic;
the end will justify everything" (ibid., p. 843). He declines to
heed the dire prediction made by his old friends d'Arthez and
Chrestien with a refusal so blatant that one doubts if it is
sincere. His falsity merely shows up the logic and justice of the
prediction. This is another example of Balzac's constant effort
to reveal the mainsprings of his fiction. The character is juxta-
posed against the greater truth which operates above the novel,
controlling destiny and making final judgments.

The reader knows that the "higher order of logic" to which
Lucien so grandly refers is nothing more than his own egotistical
scramble for success. If he could totally dedicate himself to this
program he might have a chance for success, but weak Lucien
is a victim of serious second thoughts. "Lucien remained pensive
and sad for a few moments" (ibid., p. 844). The hesitation of

Lucien, we notice, is shorter than before, and we are spared the tears of regret. Instead, Coralie arrives to reassure him that he is wise and clever. While it becomes increasingly easy for Lucien to part with his scruples, the dismissal of scruples is not an advantage in his case. He is too weak to respect the rule of honor among thieves that operates even in the world of the liberal journalists.

His polished exterior, once an asset, becomes another disadvantage. Lucien has gone too far and shone too brightly. He has become liable to the envy of other men. Most world conquerors employ strength to reach positions in which they attract adversaries, and they can rely upon this strength in the ensuing struggle, during which they attempt to make secure their position. Lucien, on the other hand, has no real right to his perch. He arrives there by a feat of legerdemain, coupled with a flashy mise-en-scène. Finally, however, he reaches a point where magic and beauty are of little or no use. The real force demanded by the situation is lacking. Thus it is that Lucien's defeat is quick and complete; his reputation, inflated like a shiny balloon, bursts at the slightest pinprick. Instead of ennobling himself through great challenge, Lucien succumbs to its unbearable cruciality.

The same kind of crucial moment is faced by the writer, Raoul Nathan, in *Une Fille d'Eve*. Nathan embarks upon a political career without the store of will that such a career demands. He pursues it like a dilettante, floundering, stepping on the wrong toes, making the wrong decisions. His entrance into the political game shows supreme disregard for its exigencies. He chooses his party using the same doubtful criteria that influence Lucien. Attracted to the strength of the moment, without thoroughly analyzing the political situation, he picks the party that he thinks will benefit him most. Since he is politically inept, his attitude is unrealistic and juvenile. Nathan becomes a pawn in the hands of more powerful and wiser men, and like Lucien, gives up the shaping of his own destiny through weakness.

One of the most successful examples of character juxtaposition is found at the end of this novel. Here Balzac exploits the technique in order to achieve a memorable conclusion, one that is dramatic, visual, ironic, and pitiless. The shock value produced by such a variety of qualities befits the nature of a conclusion. The author seeks to distill from the life of Nathan one moment that summarizes the futility of his existence and the low estate to which he has sunk through successive failures. Balzac juxtaposes Nathan upon himself. Through the eyes of Marie de Vandenesse, the woman who formerly loved him, the defeated Nathan is clearly and violently perceived in contrast with his former, flashy self. It is her love that Nathan sought and almost attained, and its destruction permits a kind of judgment peculiar to the situation.

> A man to whom a woman is indifferent, is already passably ugly in her eyes; but when she no longer loves him, he seems horrible, especially when he resembles Nathan. . . . Today, this once ambitious man, so rich in ink and so poor in will power, has capitulated and settled into the sinecure of a mediocre existence. (*Une Fille d'Eve, 2,* 168)

The kind of lucidity exercised by a woman fallen out of love is evoked for two reasons. First, its quality is exceptionally sharp, suggesting a standard and a vantage point for the reader. Balzac can hardly be accused of sentimentalizing failure, and the thoroughly detached attitude of Marie de Vandenesse is the one that he himself shares and hopes to transmit to his public. Secondly, this final reference to love is consistent with the terms in which the hero has been presented. Nathan's ambitions were stimulated by his love for Marie de Vandenesse; his defeat was brought about by his mismanaging of that love. His failure in love coincides with his failure in life; his mediocrity as a man in love indicates his fate as a mediocre human being. Balzac thus interiorizes the progression toward failure, charting its course with referents intimately related to the character's personality. The allusion to a woman's eyes brings Nathan into painful contiguity with the locus of his flaw.

In his infinitely detailed portrait of Lucien, Balzac resorts to a vast repertoire of images to suggest the character's weakness. Often, he uses timeworn clichés with telling effect, as he searches to vary the novel's point of view. His own judgments about the hero, both explicit and couched in symbols, are liberally mixed with judgments made by other characters. Balzac is careful not to betray these characters by overestimating their capacities for literary invention or by transgressing the boundaries of conversational verisimilitude. He successfully shuttles Lucien between two worlds. The character lives within his fictional reality and is abstracted for the author's privileged consideration. Lucien's weakness is obvious to Balzac, the reader, and the other characters in *Illusions perdues*. His contemporaries refer to him in terms that readily describe his flaw. Finot says to him: "In this affair, you have had the innocence of a lamb" (*Illusions perdues*, p. 862). This is pathetically true. Lucien cannot be accused of malice, only weakness and stupidity. A short while later, Claude Vignon accurately describes Lucien's shortcomings in disarmingly simple terms. "Indeed, one must be a great man to keep the balance between genius and character. Talent grows, the heart dries up. Unless one is a colossus, unless one has the shoulders of Hercules, one is left without a heart or without talent. You are thin and slender, you will succumb" (ibid., p. 873). Using familiar physical terms, Vignon states a fact that the reader has known for a long time, having had the chance to see all the contradictions in Lucien's character, all the impulses that jar against each other and are thus neutralized. In a sense, the struggle that is waged within the soul of Lucien renders him impotent for the struggle that he must wage against

the world at large. He is always pushed slightly out of tune with
the requirements of his current role, unbalanced by inner conflicts that have no bearing on the world's reality. His physique,
his expression, his bearing, and his actions reveal this to friends
and enemies alike.

Balzac feels the need to rivet Lucien's failure in the solid and
constant, if many-faceted, substructure of character reflection
that functions in the novel. At each stage in Lucien's career
another image is projected upon him, lighting up his weakness
through contrast, similarity, irony, paradox, and a number of
other tonalities. All the important characters in the novel serve
this purpose. Lucien is more a reflection of David Séchard,
Madame de Bargeton, d'Arthez, Nathan, and Lousteau than a
freestanding figure. Balzac is unwilling to surrender so important a character to the static state implied in traditional portraiture. Lucien must carry the weight of *Illusions perdues,* and
the author finds a method of characterization that at once gives
impetus and cohesion to the novel. Both the novel and the characterization gain from this connecting process. Lucien is the
moving canvas upon which is painted the gamut of social life
in the provinces and in Paris. In this he resembles Rastignac, the
key to the city's many levels. The diverse arenas described in
novels like *Illusions perdues* and *Le Père Goriot* are made to fit
comfortably in consistent schemes and become tangential
through the use of ubiquitous dandies. The author carries the
technique one step further when he orients each arena to illustrate a particular aspect of the chameleon-like protagonist.

At the end of "Un Grand homme de province à Paris" Coralie
is Lucien's most important referent. Through the linking device
of love and honesty, Balzac amalgamates the destinies of these
two characters. During the second part of *Illusions perdues* he
posits their relationship in these terms, drawing them closer to
each other as he separates them from society. This relationship
gives an unusual color to the hero's weakness. Its inception

illustrates a basic paradox. Lucien yearns for Coralie in spite of the fact that she already has a protector. "After having shown Lousteau the profoundest distaste for this most odious sharing, he fell into the ditch, he swam in desire, drawn on by the jesuitism of passion" (ibid., p. 722). Balzac continuously places his hero in such predicaments, exaggerating his intention with linguistic connotations of weakness and confusion. Having fallen into the proverbial ditch and helpless so to speak, it is no surprise that Lucien's love is born in the shadow of compromise, hypocrisy, and weakness. Prepared to take a mistress who is being kept by another man, he is prey to a fleeting desire, the passion of a moment, the superficial attraction of beauty. It is Balzac's ever-present irony that makes Coralie's love for Lucien pure and self-sacrificing, belying its questionable beginnings. Paradoxically, the actress shows the poet what constitutes real love. He is fortunate enough to happen upon a woman who, in spite of her superficial inappropriateness for a poet's love, proves to be more worthy than this particular poet deserves.

Balzac compounds this irony with another strange twist. The true love of Coralie proves to be just as fatal to Lucien as insincerity would have been. Simply falling in love is Lucien's great mistake, for his liaison will prove to be a serious liability in his career. Lucien's love is the only example of unselfishness permitted him by Balzac. His liaison with Madame de Bargeton smacks of opportunism, and his family affections are feeble indeed. Only Coralie manages to command lasting allegiance, drawing from the poet sacrifices and true sentiments. Balzac is determined to endow this affair with great sincerity, thus emphasizing the falsity upon which it impinges. The first element of this falsity is the artificiality implicit in Lucien and explicit in Coralie. She notices the similarity of their professions but does not comprehend their capacity for overnight success and overnight failure. This susceptibility stems, of course, from the weakness inherent in the nature of their falsity.

The reader is prepared to see in Coralie's fiasco a prediction of Lucien's imminent defeat. Since they are mirror images, even in their beauty, the author can count on the reader making such an inference. Coralie dies, and Lucien must write ribald drinking songs to finance her funeral. The love is foully besmirched by the society that ordained its destruction.

The author, constantly aware of the overtones contained within the resonance of the Coralie-Lucien identity, extracts perhaps the most resounding one upon which to resolve Lucien's Parisian sojourn. Crushed under the weight of his woes, the poet looks to the Seine and suicide for escape. This is not less than one would expect from a romantic poet in such an unhappy situation. But since the author has decided to allow Lucien to proceed to new deceits and new treacheries, it would not be fitting to allow sympathy to distort the reader's judgment. Balzac must somehow efface the small moment of strength afforded Lucien in his grief. The prospective suicide is averted by the intervention of Bérénice, Coralie's maid, who convinces him to continue living and, furthermore, prostitutes herself to finance his ignominious retreat to Angoulême. This act of prostitution is the grand gesture that terminates Lucien's eventful season in Paris. Balzac is simply unable to resist the pungent irony found in Bérénice's sacrifice. The noble, generous prostitute saves the weak, ineffectual, and treacherous one. The symbolism of this act cannot be lost upon Lucien, who has, in effect, sold his soul to Paris. At the end of this section, Lucien and the reader are left with a horrible reminder of the depths to which he has fallen.

The symmetry traced by the development of Lucien's Parisian sojourn is completed. He begins with nothing and ends with nothing. The progress of his career describes a semicircle, with the hero weakly seeking to climb upward and, because of his weakness, falling back to the level from which he started. One might think that Lucien actually sinks lower, since he is voided of his illusions and his aspirations, but this is not exactly true. We see in the next section of the novel that the rubber-faced hero is ready to start all over again. His moral baggage is light at the beginning of his journey, and it becomes lighter in Paris, but not enough to discourage him from continuing on in search of the elusive glory that keeps slipping from his grasp.

In the third part of *Illusions perdues,* Lucien relinquishes the major role to David Séchard but still manages to arrest much of the reader's attention. Balzac transports his hero back to Angoulême, and it is there that his character is further plumbed to reveal the extent of his weakness. He is finally stripped bare of a will and thus becomes a fit partner for the master puppeteer, Vautrin-Herrera-Collin. This will prove to be the ultimate human failure.

Irony is the device most often used by Balzac to characterize Lucien during the course of "Les Souffrances de l'inventeur." This irony depends upon a direction announced in the previous sections of *Illusions perdues* and best described as treason to art. This is perhaps Lucien's most heinous crime in the eyes of Balzac, the vengeful keeper of the flame. The useless sacrifice of his novel met with Balzac's vehement judgment. Having degraded the literary profession through the neglect of his talent as well as through his allegiance to journalism, Lucien earns for himself scorn and is caricaturized as a fatuous poet. Balzac does not miss an opportunity to focus this useful cliché upon his squirming protagonist. Each of Lucien's decisions and actions are immediately reduced to comic poses, with the result that the character becomes progressively flattened. This is the author's intention, and we shall see the fruits borne by this method.

At the beginning of "Les Souffrances de l'inventeur," Lucien covers himself with reproach upon discovering the effect that his forgery has had on the Séchard family. This is the poet's usual reaction to feelings of guilt, and we are not surprised to learn that he turns them into a poem. "And Lucien told of his misfortunes. When he had finished reciting this poem in a

manner truly worthy of a poet" (ibid., p. 885). Lucien's mind
is facile, and his lamentation soon becomes an excuse for self-
glorification in the poeticizing of sorrow. Balzac is merciless.
He never lets the reader forget that Lucien is incapable of sincere contrition, incapable of bearing the weight of his guilt.
Every sentiment is reduced to its basic ingredient of comic-opera
saccharine. And it is with a comic-opera fanfare that he returns
to Angoulême. "His heart still palpitating from the remorse
awakened in him by the story of the old priest, he accepted this
punishment for the moment, having decided to brave the stares
of people he knew. He said to himself, 'I am heroic!' " (ibid.,
p. 969) Lucien returns to Angoulême with full knowledge of
the damage he has caused his family and his old friend, David
Séchard, with the kind of remorse he has always felt, with the
kind of conscience that allows him to bear any humiliation.
He returns because he has nowhere else to go. His entry into the
city, in rags, is turned into an occasion for self-congratulation.
Only a man completely lacking in courage could find comfort
in this pitiful self-deceit.

Balzac manipulates Lucien's vulnerability to praise and his
bent for poetic postures to advance the plot of the last part of
Illusions perdues. The enemies of David Séchard blind Lucien
into complicity with their blandishments of glory, and he betrays his friend once more. This realization does not shock
Lucien into a cognizance of reality, but rather it gives him the
chance to play a great scene of farewell, write a note in despera-
tion, vent his sorrow in tones befitting a romantic poet. He
resolves to leave his family, indulging in a letter of self-reproach and breast-beating. "Ah well! I am the marked one in
our family" (ibid., p. 1010). An artist to the bitter end, he in-
vokes the tragic destiny that has haunted his career. A man of
courage would have left no letter at all, but Lucien is weak
enough to express his self-pity in the most blatant of hyperboles.
"O my dear Eve, I judge myself more severely than anyone, for
I condemn myself absolutely and without pity" (ibid., p. 1011).

After such a confession, he proceeds to enumerate the factors that shaped his behavior. This is the extent of his lack of pity.

Lucien points most willingly to his artistic temperament in this letter to his sister. He has two motives in doing so. First, he shunts the responsibility of his actions onto the fatal make-up of his personality, thereby exonerating his nonexistent will. In effect, he states that his destiny is determined by the lack of equilibrium found in the artistic type. Secondly, he allies himself with a group that constitutes an elite, a group that is entitled to a special brand of pity. Thus, Lucien can satisfy his need for self-importance. We are not surprised to see him trying to satisfy such a need, indulging in his usual tragic-hero histrionics. Even at the depths of his despair, crumbling under the realization of the sorrow he has wrought, he reveals the truth of his personality by his inability to discard the caricature.

Lucien strikes a melodramatic tone in this letter. He announces his suicide, but the reader is less convinced now than he was at the end of "Un Grand homme de province à Paris." Here, he clothes his death sentence in declamatory garb, robbing it of sincerity. " 'Yes, I have decided. Farewell then forever, my dear Eve. I feel some sweetness in thinking that I will go on living only in your hearts. There my tomb will be . . . I do not wish for any other one. Farewell again! . . . It is your brother's last' " (ibid., p. 1012). The exaggerated finality of this farewell and the sentimental reference to living on in the memory of the survivors are deftly contrived effects that further Balzac's purpose. He is determined to present an uncompromising portrait of Lucien de Rubempré, one so painted that the character's decisions and actions throughout a two-novel career will be judged without inconsistency. One might be tempted to allow Lucien to salvage some vestige of the reader's pity, but Balzac ruthlessly denies him this luxury and, through the use of diction, lets the reader penetrate the hero's miserable confession.

As if one could have missed the intention of the farewell letter, the author continues to satirize Lucien's suicide attempt, always in terms of the poetic pose. "Once his resolution was taken, Lucien fell into a deliberation on the means to effectuate it, and the poet wanted a poetic end" (ibid., p. 1013). The reader can justifiably question Lucien's will to die, a desire ridiculously tempered by his external pride. He searches for the proper place for his drowning, one designed for a handsome young poet who is loath to have his bloated corpse on public exhibition. "He had, as some suicides do, a posthumous *amour-propre*" (ibid., p. 1013). Finally, he comes upon the ideal spot, and his remark injects a shaft of macabre humor into the novel, revealing Balzac's intention. "There is a spot which makes your mouth water for a drowning, the poet said to himself while admiring this lovely little country vista" (ibid., p. 1014).

We have stressed the manner in which Balzac circumscribes the delineation of Lucien within human boundaries through the repeated devices of reflection, overt judgments made by other characters, and self-consciousness. Nowhere is the author's unwillingness to translate portraiture into extra-human terms seen to greater advantage than at the end of *Illusions perdues.* Having firmly rooted Lucien's malady in his defective *volonté,* Balzac is now ready to dramatize, with the directness we have come to expect, the final act of self-treason. By capitalizing upon Lucien's self-awareness, his penchant for self-expression, his willingness to indulge in self-apostrophization, he places the eloquent failure once more before the truth. From the resulting contact can be extracted a full realization of this character's relationship to the world, the reasons for his downfall, the extent of his disease. "Instead of killing myself, I have sold my life. I no longer belong to myself, I am more than a secretary to a Spanish diplomat, I am his creature" (ibid., p. 1048). Lucien makes this confession in a letter to his sister Eve, and we are reminded of the novel's first pages, where Eve was described as representing all that is steadfast, loyal, good, and honest. She is a double of her husband, David Séchard, and the qualities of this couple put into vivid relief the short-comings of Lucien. Their close relationship with him—David, a spiritual brother, and Eve, a blood sister—further emphasizes all that Lucien should be, by placing within this family intimacy those poles so cherished by Balzac, good and bad, black and white. It is perhaps this duality of Lucien's nature that forces him into an awareness of his act. When he writes to Eve, he is writing to another part of himself, and as he writes, he reacts with her indignation. But in spite of indignation, in spite of awareness, he submits. This is the most important clue to the state of Lucien's *volonté.* In the second part of the novel he saw his own fate in the person of Raoul Nathan and through greed, decided to risk his life. Selling himself to Vautrin, knowing full well the implications of this act, Lucien demon-strates the fact that he has been totally voided of will. He has no choice. Unable to function for himself, submission to another will is the only posture left to him.

Balzac has, in a sense, discarded the character of Lucien. He has brought him through the peripeties of a shameful career, very much the worse for wear. The plot of *Illusions perdues* has emptied him of personality, and the author can safely heap ridicule upon this anti-heroic figure. The reader no longer be-lieves in him as a person for Balzac has purposely destroyed this belief. What remains is an attractive physical shell, the personification of weakness. Throughout the novel we have witnessed the shredding of the character's soul, until virtually no soul is left. We have seen the fabrication of a human marion-ette, the shape that Lucien is about to assume. He is ripe to fall into the incredibly powerful hands of the most strong-willed character in *La Comédie humaine,* Vautrin. The story of their relationship, *Splendeurs et misères des courtisanes,* is not the story of two human beings. It is rather an allegory that demon-strates the effect of strength upon weakness. The failure of Lucien in *Illusions perdues* is the failure of the weak man. The failure of Lucien in *Splendeurs et misères des courtisanes* is the failure of weakness. One can accept the complete prostitution of Lucien's will in the second novel without flinching because Lucien, as a character, no longer demands compassion or respect. He has put on a mask and proceeds to act out a part in a play, directed by an outer force and relieved of responsibility for his actions. The process of character reflection, so carefully traced in *Illusions perdues,* is brought to culmination in the later novel, where Lucien is turned into a mirror.

The respective roles of Lucien and Vautrin are disclosed to us in the first pages of *Splendeurs et misères des courtisanes.* At an opera ball Lucien astonishes the spectators with his beauty. Vautrin follows close behind, hidden in a domino. Lucien is the face; Vautrin is the strength. In a variety of guises, the ex-convict directs the career of his young protégé, planning his every move, imparting to Lucien a success he could never manage to garner for himself. Vautrin uses the attractive shield of Lucien in a grasp for power, as he assaults the stronghold that is society. "Old men in whom the active aspect of life has been displaced, and has been transported into the sphere of personal interest, often feel the need of a pretty machine, of a young and passionate actor to accomplish their projects" (*Splendeurs et misères des courtisanes,* 5, 697). Vautrin cannot participate directly in a worldly life. He is a marked man, whose face and history are too well known. What better method is left to him than the occupation of another man's soul? To accomplish this Vautrin needed to find a being who, through lack of a soul, could conceivably be inhabited. Lucien is a perfect victim. "He had himself represented in social life by this poet, to whom he gave his consistency and his will of iron" (ibid., p. 725).

Since Lucien has abdicated his will, he is naturally deprived of his formerly revealing capacity for self-awareness and self-expression. It is through the eyes of the other characters that the author must finish his portrait. In effect, there is no longer a need to discuss the interior of Lucien's being, for it has ceased to exist. Esther, the woman he loves, is his most poignant judge. Realizing that Lucien is ready to discard her simply because Vautrin tells him to, she understands the extent of the criminal's domination over her lover. This aspect of the relationship between Lucien and Vautrin is more shocking than their fundamental sexual abnormality which plays so strong a role in the novel. Balzac does not resort to Svengali–Trilby trappings of hypnotism and black magic; Lucien does not sell his soul to the devil, but to another human being. One can understand Esther's reaction to the moral self-betrayal committed by Lucien and the shameless possession indulged in by Vautrin. Esther is the first to join the reader in witnessing the enactment of this marionette show. At the opera ball, Rastignac may have had an inkling of the true situation, seeing Vautrin's machinations and remembering the famous garden conversation he had with the ex-convict in *Le Père Goriot*. Esther, however, is allowed to see Lucien groveling before the cassocked arch-villain, unabashedly demonstrating the extent of his weakness.

Another device used to measure Lucien is the imposition of a former image of himself upon his present being. Balzac juxtaposes the ambitious young poet-novelist and the helpless pawn with chilling effect. Lucien has forgotten his old pretensions and abandoned his old dreams and attitudes. In *Illusions perdues* his greatest desire was to become the literary sensation of Paris. By a stroke of fate, this comes to pass; his novel and his collection of poems enjoy a great success. But this leaves him unmoved; he calls it a "posthumous success" (ibid., p. 711). Such a remark, made flippantly, contains more than a germ of truth. At the end of *Illusions perdues,* Vautrin prevented Lucien's physical death but instead caused a spiritual one. Nothing is left of the aspiring poet, the idealistic student, the impulsive fortune seeker. These visages of Lucien are effaced, sacrificed to the masterplan of Vautrin. There is no true visage in their place, only the cold brilliance of a mirror. We know that

Lucien has assumed another man's personality because he is
prepared to await the victory of "the patient politician."

The extent of Vautrin's domination over Lucien is no surprise. The foulest compromise and the most cowardly treachery
are now perfectly consistent with Lucien's character. He no
longer hesitates between right and wrong, strength or weakness, because he has discarded his power of choice. This is no
more startlingly seen than in his betrayal of Esther, the woman
he has adored for four years. At the propitious moment, Vautrin
decides that Esther must be sold to the banker Nucingen, in
order to finance the furtherance of Lucien's career. Lucien is
unable to make even a feeble gesture in opposition to the
superior will of Vautrin. One of Balzac's favorite clichés deftly
portrays the power wielded by Vautrin. The initiated reader
of *La Comédie humaine* immediately recognizes in the glance
of the master an irresistible dose of *volonté*.

> Then he riveted upon Lucien one of his fixed and penetrat-
> ing glances which makes the will of strong men enter
> into the souls of the weak. This fascinating glance, which
> had for its effect the collapse of all resistance, announced
> between Lucien and his counselor not only secrets of life
> and death, but feelings as superior to ordinary feelings as
> this man was to the lowliness of his position. (ibid., p. 725)

Balzac constantly employs the eyes as an organizing factor.
It is through the eyes that two beings meet, the observer and the
object observed. By stressing such moments of cognizance, the
author manages to make especially clear the opposing characteristics of both factors. The eyes of Marie de Vandenesse
provide such a focus at the end of *Une Fille d'Eve*. Balzac goes
one step further in *Splendeurs et misères des courtisanes,* since
it is the power emanating from Vautrin's eyes that distinguishes
him from Lucien and thoroughly defines Lucien's weakness.
Vautrin is a superman, whose stature increases when seen in
conjunction with his own low station and Lucien's nonentity.

It is unnecessary to chronicle the events that mark Lucien's second Parisian career since he plays in them only a shadow-like role. In the third section of the novel, however, "Où Mènent les mauvais chemins," Lucien is separated from Vautrin and thereby reintroduced to himself. In this moment of crisis, he becomes the Lucien of *Illusions perdues*, feminine, sensitive, impractical. Pridefully, he denies the contention that Herrera-Collin-Vautrin is his father, reveals the truth about their relationship, is honest when he might just as easily lie to save his skin. Lucien's judgment is again destroyed by his affections and his sentiments. In his weakness, he is profoundly moved by Esther's deathbed letter, just as he was shackled by his love for Coralie in *Illusions perdues*. Crushed by his betrayal of Vautrin and by the extent of Esther's self-sacrifice, Lucien dissolves into tears, his usual reaction to life's difficulties. He is galvanized into action, however, by the fear of having to meet Vautrin. This, more than despair or shame, strengthens Lucien's resolve to commit suicide. In these last moments of Lucien's life, Balzac once again demonstrates the double utility of character reflection. As a method of portraiture, the final reference to Vautrin serves as a reminder that Lucien's capacity for a relationship with such a man lies at the root of his weakness. As a method of novelistic organization, it is a recurrent theme, a memory point, a familiar sign in the vast world of these two sprawling novels.

Paradoxically, Lucien finds strength in the weakness of his cowardice. This time the reader knows that suicide will not be another vain attempt, the desire of a passing moment, the balm for Lucien's short-lived despair. Gone are the sighs of self-pity, the hestitations, the rhetoric of romantic poetry. With a good deal of lucidity and resolve, Lucien manages to accomplish the feat of killing himself. His suicide comes as a relief and is perhaps the one forceful act in his life. In the eyes of the law, Lucien deserves to live, but in the eyes of the Balzacian universe, he is unfit to survive. Tired of living on borrowed time, he ex-

terminates himself, thereby putting to an end slow progress of
his failure. The primitive forces at work in the world long ago
decreed his defeat.

There is, however, another way of interpreting Lucien's
catastrophic end. Vautrin, the spokesman for Balzac's materialistic philosophy, expresses it with clarity. "In this fighter's profession, when you have a good hand, and the opening play,
the candle falls down, the cards burn, or the player is stricken
with a heart attack! . . . That is the story of Lucien, this boy,
this angel, who did not commit the shadow of a crime; *il s'est
laissé faire, il a laissé faire!*" (ibid., p. 1136). Vautrin suggests
that Lucien's defeat was brought about by a chance combination of events, which is, of course, absolutely true. In our first
chapter we discussed Balzac's understanding of the illogical
make-up of the universe. But he does assert that this patternless
set of circumstances which comprises one individual's moment
in time can be mastered by a great man, and there is proof of
this in *La Comédie humaine.* Vautrin, who so bitterly describes
the chance train of events that spells the doom of Lucien, possesses the attributes that enable one to triumph over life's confusion. Able to wield the tools of perspicacity, fortitude, and
self-malleability, he is supremely gifted in the art of succeeding.
His judgment of Lucien would have been more accurate if he
had emphasized the statement, "il s'est laissé faire." This is
perhaps Lucien's most unpardonable crime. It is reflected in the
very title of the novel, *Splendeurs et misères des courtisanes.*
Esther the prostitute is the alter ego for Lucien the prostitute,
just as Coralie the actress reflected Lucien the actor. The author
has a gift for title invention, and in this title he reveals more
than one initially suspects. Lucien sells himself into submission, committing total prostitution. In prostituting himself to
Vautrin, he prostitutes himself to the world at large. When a
man falls one step behind the seething current that is his
existence, when he gives in to confusion for a fraction of a
second, he is doomed by a system that permits the survival of

only the strong. Lucien is always incongruent to his moment. Despite an ability to contort his face to meet the requirements of a variety of events, he lacks that special quality of truly merging with time. His shams are superficial compromises, and he is ultimately rejected by the machine, which calls for domination rather than accommodation. It is the lot of the superman, Vautrin, whose intelligence fully comprehends the moment, whose presence fills it, and whose will shapes it, to succeed. The criminal turns policeman.

CHAPTER 5

Genius: The Word's Dilemma

Balzac, the least overtly autobiographical of novelists, has painfully assassinated extensions of his personal idealism in novels like *Illusions perdues, César Birotteau,* and *Le Père Goriot.* The world conqueror, the good, the loving are all sent to their ordained defeats with more than a slight flinch of self-recognition on the part of the author. This is, of course, the true measure of his realism, and it is a realism much more sweeping than the illusion of physical reality. It is a fact of life. Balzac, the judge and victim, pursues relentlessly the better part of himself, mitigating any gesture of hope for the human kind with the cutting guillotine-lorgnette of Henri de Marsay-Balzac, the soulless observer. Yet nowhere is the ambiguity of his attitude more apparent than in his treatment of the genius figure. Throughout *La Comédie humaine,* the great man looms up out of the crowd and is then quickly eliminated by the voracious machine. The genius represents all of the author's aspirations, his belief in the force of the idea, his fervent conviction that men can be god-like, artistic, and therefore transcend themselves.[1] The dual nature of failure emerges from the fate of

1. Maurice Beebe, in "The Lesson of Balzac's Artists," *Criticism,* 2 (1960), 221–41, examines the transference of the author's own visage and preoccupations to the artist figures in *La Comédie humaine.* Mr. Beebe

Louis Lambert, Gambara, Claës, and Frenhofer. The whole concept of failure must be reevaluated in the light of their existence, for then failure reveals the circumference of Balzac's plotting of the world.

Louis Lambert is undoubtedly the most fascinating of the geniuses of the "Études philosophiques." The resemblance between the child prodigy, miraculously discovered on the banks of the Loire by Madame de Staël, and the precocious, philosophically inclined young Balzac is well known. The author's unhappy schoolboy experiences in Tours find expression in Lambert's solitude and castigation. Lambert's life describes an accelerating concentration of self-consciousness, a refinement of the will through Idea, and the eventual immersion within the new world of the Word. This is demonstrated in the list of aphorisms which closes the novel. The philosopher has succeeded in achieving the summit of creativity, has become the most poetic of poets by condensing World into Word. This is not a process of transformation, but rather one of substitution. The kingdom of angels is relevant to Louis Lambert's perception, and the logic of his statement that angels are white is a most rational statement of fact. In extreme terms, the alienation of Lambert is parallel to the artistic process and, in particular, to the creation of *La Comédie humaine.* As Albert Béguin so clearly demonstrates, the relationship between the descriptions found in Balzac's novels and any observable reality is coincidental and of relatively small importance.[2] The objects that clutter the rooms of fictional

---

discusses certain ambiguities in the artist in *Ivory Towers and Sacred Founts, the Artist as Hero in Fiction from Goethe to Joyce* (New York, 1964), pp. 175–96.

2. Albert Béguin's *Balzac visionnaire* (Geneva, 1946) is a fascinating analysis of symbolic, magical reality in *La Comédie humaine.* "The real world only appears so real because it is the transparent surface of the other world. One truly has the feeling of being *in life,* but one would not always feel this if the tangible were not always the symbol and the manifestation

life are conjured from the deepest recesses of the author's imagination and are the accouterments of the other world he seeks to describe. This other world is graphically detailed; in fact, the accumulation of details heightens its otherworldliness. The Pension Vauquer becomes less and less real in proportion to the number of observations made by the author in the first pages of *Le Père Goriot*. Increasingly it becomes the house of magic, the place of hallucination that is the fitting center of this novel's universe. As such, it is just as much a substitute world as is Louis Lambert's heaven. The spiritual fraternity of Lambert and Balzac, first manifested in the similarity of their adolescent years and then by their mutual tendency to achieve a unification of all existence within the Word, reaches its fullest expression in this common act of substitution. Balzac writes *La Comédie humaine;* Lambert loses his mind. It is their different solutions that interest us, for it makes tangential the author's views on failure, as well as certain aspects of his aesthetics.

The first page of *Louis Lambert* contains the now-familiar preparation for what is to follow. Lambert as a child is a special creature, already showing signs of impatience with worldly existence, already seeking escape into a different sphere.

> Did this infantile imagination already understand the mysterious profundity of the Scriptures, could it already follow the Holy Spirit in its flight across worlds, did it only become enticed by the romantic attractions which abound in these oriental poems; or, in its first innocence, did this soul sympathize with the religious sublimity that

---

of the invisible. For life, as the naturalists grossly believed, is not limited to its immediate appearance. It is life only when all around it, above and beneath, on top, on the bottom and especially at its interior, one divines or perceives something which goes beyond it. In order to thus see life in its true reality, one must, even more than for evoking dreams, be endowed with visionary powers" (pp. 76–77).

divine hands poured into this book? (*Louis Lambert*, 10, 353)

The Bible, with its exotic, oriental promise of heaven, with its description of a supralogical existence, greatly appeals to the imaginative young Lambert, avidly searching for an expression of the eternal other, that special beyond that will belong to him alone. He has begun his journey to the land in which he will perceive the whiteness of angels, and it is a journey propelled by a world that he is eager to leave and that in turn is eager to be rid of him.[3] This is what distinguishes Lambert and his genius counterparts in *La Comédie humaine* from the failures of Lucien de Rubempré, Birotteau, Lousteau, Nathan, and even Baron Hulot. The existence of the latter group depends, in varying degrees, on the world at large. Recognition, monetary gain, and pleasures of the flesh demand a participation in, and are defined by, the community of men. Lambert asks for nothing from this community; in fact, he scorns it. This enables Balzac to work out a strange formula, in which the hero enjoys the fullest success and the most resounding failure. There is no attempt made to resolve this paradox. It is, instead, the most faithful reproduction of the author's moral predicament as he is forced to condemn the hero-artist-genius. Lambert tastes the sweetest pyrrhic victory, one made sweeter by the completeness of the defeat dealt him by the world. Again we are plunged into the magnetic field of opposites dear to the author and, as we have seen, a constant source for his rhetoric. Failure becomes the mirror image of success, for it is success turned backward. Fundamentally, for Louis Lambert failure in the eyes of the world means personal success. Each step away from the sphere of men is one step nearer the kingdom of heaven.

3. Georges Poulet, in "La Distance intérieure," *Études sur le temps humain* (Paris, 1952), 11, comments on the time and space voyages of Lambert in an effort to underline a tension between freedom of thought and a perception of the fixity of existence.

Of course, the god in this heaven is Louis Lambert, and the angels are a fraternity of soul mates of his own creation. The similarity between Balzac the author-god and Lambert the philosopher-god is fundamental and goes deep in explaining the former's liberation from the constricts of observed reality. As Balzac peers within objects and yields true form from unyielding physicality, Lambert discovers the mechanism of the divine ticking in the near, yet distant, reaches of space. They are both fascinated by the powers of the Word, imparting an intrinsic existence to the symbol and seeking to find in the symbol the clue to the truth for which they search.

> "I have often gone," he said to me, in speaking of his readings, "on delightful voyages, embarked on a word into the depths of the past. . . . What a beautiful book one might compose in telling the life and adventures of a word! Without a doubt it has received diverse impressions from the events which it has served." (ibid., p. 355)

Lambert goes on to examine the properties of the word "vrai," discussing its shape and sonic qualities. The transition between this and the history of all human knowledge is easily made; the key has been found; and in Lambert's fantastications about the Word, the universe is compressed. The delightful voyages to which he alludes are analogous to Balzac's journeys through fiction, exploring the universe through the minutia of the Pension Vauquer, the complete title of *César Birotteau,* or the passe-partout of Vautrin's character. The author literally pounces upon the Word and turns it inside out in an effort to illuminate the entrance to the great maze of life. The reader follows obediently, armed with the magic thread, never losing his way along a path strewn with signals from the guide. The particular resonance of the Balzacian signal, the importance of the face, the name, the antithesis, the paradox, becomes increasingly familiar as the center of the maze is neared, and in this way, *La Comédie humaine* inevitably becomes one novel to the reader who has the courage and stamina necessary to finish the journey. He is initiated, and all the irrationality becomes just as meaningful as the whiteness of Lambert's angels. The true world has failed, is scorned in favor of the fictional one, and Balzac has achieved his greatest success as an artist.

The excitement of invention and world building that pulses through *La Comédie humaine* draws its source of energy from the author's constant willingness to leave behind accepted patterns of reality. This is what distinguishes Balzac from the realists and naturalists. He never hesitates before a digression, because he knows instinctively that the seeming digression is truly an amplification of his substitute world, which reflects light back upon the real world he is ostensibly describing. His joy in description, in the feel and weight of the words on paper, reveals his desire to transmit a world of his own creation. In this act of creation his humanity is exalted, like that of Louis Lambert. "His brain, accustomed at an early age to the difficult mechanism of concentrating human energy, drew from this rich deposit a swarm of wonderful images of reality, of freshness, with which he nourished himself during his lucid contemplations" (ibid., p. 357). By concentrating these human forces of intelligence and will power, Lambert hurtles himself upward, with the image as a spring. The unity of his being in this concentration is imposed upon the unity of the universe and is akin to the creative process. There is, however, one important distinction. Balzac is hurtled through the image into the communication of art. He thrusts himself into an intellectual immediacy with the world, embodied in readers, while Lambert follows the opposite course. "When he thus employed all his power in reading, he in some way lost consciousness of his physical life, and existed only through the all-powerful play of his interior organs whose influence had been immeasurably extended: as he used to say, he left *space behind*" (ibid., p. 358). This soaring through space, this leaving behind of space, cuts Lambert off from other men. There is a mutual process of exclusion. He is suffocated by the putrid air of the school, by its dirt, by its inflexible rules. The physical misery of his surroundings makes the flight just that much more necessary. Yet the flight upward emphasizes the squalor of that which is abandoned, and the consciousness of such squalor is intolerable to those who create it. Thus, Lambert reminds mediocre men of their mediocrity, is a menace to their self-esteem, and must therefore be destroyed. That which is different is feared. The narrator and Lambert become scapegoats for both the teachers and the students, simply because they remain apart.

> The Poet-and-Pythagoras was thus an exception, a life outside of the common life. That instinct of schoolboys which is so penetrating, that very delicate *amour-propre* made some sense in us spirits situated higher than theirs, and others, spirits which were inferior. That produced, in the former, a hatred for our mute aristocracy, in the latter, disdain for our uselessness. (ibid., p. 377)

Here is reflected society's ambivalent attitude toward the great man, rejected for his superiority, ostracized for his inferiority. The shadow cast by Louis Lambert is too long, and it is, in the last analysis, only a shadow. The rule of pragmatism is arrogantly defied. Lambert's failure is a classic example of incongruence with the great machine.

There is no alternative for Louis Lambert. He cannot come to rest in *this* sphere after one of his flights. Other men prohibit it. "This eagle, who wanted the world for a pasture, found himself between four dirty and narrow walls; in spite of this, his life became, in the broadest sense of the term, an ideal life" (ibid., p. 378). He is exiled from his native land, an exile in, of all places, a school. The irony is obvious. Organized education is the final proof of man's mediocrity. It is an institution designed to propagate nonintelligence, to choke off imagination and originality which menace the order of things. Balzac dramatizes and symbolizes this in the scene where ignorant Father

Haugoult seizes Lambert's manuscript. The boy has no right
to think creatively, to question the authority of the past with
an original contribution to the future. The priest tries to wrench
away Lambert's difference, his talent, his mind, so that he will
resemble the other schoolboys. "Father Haugoult probably
sold the *Treatise on Will* to a grocer in Vendôme, without
knowing the importance of the scientific treasures whose
aborted germs were dissipated into ignorant hands" (ibid.,
p. 388). This product of Lambert's intelligence will be used
to wrap groceries. It will be made useful and thereby debased.
Meaning is replaced by the most grossly tangible; cognition
is replaced by ignorance; the mind is replaced by the hands.

Father Haugoult is the agent of the first but not the most
significant failure in the philosopher's life. The latter is to be
found in the nature of his philosophy and in its basic uncom-
municability. In this area Balzac the idealist collides with Balzac
the artist, and the shock produced is one of the most curious
phenomena in *La Comédie humaine.*

The gist of Balzac and Lambert's Swedenborgism is conveyed by their conviction that men are inhabited by angelic
beings, that there is another side of humanity which seeks
liberation from the shell of the body. The fullest expression of
this can be found in the story of Seraphita, the androgyne.
There, the angel speaks before leaving the world. But the
ultimate goal is not expression, but flight, flight not in the least
intellectual and therefore defying logical exposition. The style
most suited to it is impressionistic and vague, suggesting mystic
transport and the ineffable beyond. The narrator of *Louis
Lambert* is well aware of this.

This doctrine, which I endeavor to summarize by giving
it a logical order, was presented to me by Lambert with
all the seductive trappings of mystery, enveloped in the
swaddling clothes of the phraseology particular to mystics:
an obscure diction, filled with abstractions, and so stimu-

lating to the brain, that there are certain books by Jacob
Boehm, by Swedenborg or by Madame Guyon whose
concentrated reading stimulates fantasies as multiform
as the dreams produced by opium. (ibid., p. 381)

This is, of course, the only diction suitable to the philosophy,
but the craftsman in Balzac, through the mouth of the narrator,
rejects it as being too difficult for his readers and perhaps even
for himself. He is reduced to a pseudo-scientific résumé of a
nonscientific experience. Balzac, whose rhetoric masters a particularly complex universe, albeit one of his own creation,
flounders unimaginatively when it comes to a logical analysis
of mysticism or, as we shall soon see, of music. Both these
domains are imposed upon the transfigured physicality that is
the stuff of *La Comédie humaine.* The mystical relationships,
the power of will, and even the musical flights of imagery work
well within the strict literary framework of the novels, but they
shrivel up when the author seeks to expose rationally their
place in his thinking. The spirit and the art are dissipated by
these futile attempts at representing what can be only simulated
or implied. The narrator's account of Lambert's treatise is a
curio, a relic of half-baked philosophizing and metaphysical
conjecture. Balzac lamely admits that he is attempting to give
order to chaos, and this is his greatest mistake. A rendering of
the chaos, at which he is elsewhere so skillful, would have been
much more eloquent. One need only examine the orgy of
words in *La Peau de chagrin* to see how successful he is in tran-
scending the Word and expressing the irrational in an irrational
way. What he does for an orgy in *La Peau de chagrin,* he does
for lust in the technicolored *La Fille aux yeux d'or.* In both
cases he is aware that the rhetoric must be suited to the fictional
matter. But his method is totally different in *Louis Lambert.*
Here, he seeks to explain the hero's alienation from the world
in basically logical terms, first in an explanation of Swedenborgism and then in the seemingly endless list of aphorisms

uttered by Lambert on those rare occasions when he leaves his catatonic state. Balzac's uneasiness in this area is painful and pathetically unnecessary. Lambert's otherworldliness is indeed conveyed, but artistically rather than philosophically. The allusion to the whiteness of angels graphically defines the boundaries of his spirit world; his childhood foresight in the episode concerning the excursion to the Manor of Rochambeau dramatizes his special gift; and the hysterical tone of his letters to Pauline de Villenoix portrays the coming of his divine madness. The compendium of his philosophical utterances is superfluous and, even worse, exceedingly dull.

Louis Lambert, as a novel, is an illuminating mistake. In it, the author flails about for a form. Nostalgic reconstruction of the past, letters, an account of Lambert's adult life refracted through a chance meeting with his uncle, the treatise, the aphorisms, and the final confrontation are all attempts to explain this basically unexplainable life. Louis Lambert is not meant to be understood. His mystery purposely excludes definition, and Balzac should have been content with leaving it so.

When the undefinable is allowed to dominate, the novel comes to life, and the character becomes convincing. These moments are closely related to Lambert's failure to find a modus vivendi, to express his philosophy and passion. He tries to convey his mystico-intellectual transports to Pauline de Villenoix, the woman he loves.

> I then envelop the world with my thought, I knead it, I fashion it, I penetrate it, I understand it or believe I understand it; but suddenly I awaken alone, and find myself in a profound night, quite puny; I forget the lights I have just seen, I am bereft of help, and especially of a heart in which I might find refuge! (ibid., p. 426)

Here we see Louis Lambert, alone with himself (as he must be inevitably), in the proverbial dark night of the soul, struggling with the monster of his own being, unable to express it or even to reconstruct its conceptualization. He has gone further away from the Word and suddenly feels alone and abandoned, a slave to himself, running madly after his own imagination. The inadequacy of language is a reversal for the Lambert who used to sail on the back of the syllable to a state of super-cognizance. He has, in effect, sailed too far, fueled by the added stimulus of love. "I wish that there were a language other than that which I use, in order to express the renascent delights of my love" (ibid., p. 434). In the agony of not finding such a language both for his ideas and for his love, he attempts self-castration, an act that can be interpreted in two ways. The most obvious seems to be a physical manifestation of the char-acter's search for freedom from the flesh, a severing of the animal from the spiritual. This is wholly consistent with the development of the character and is prefigured by the ever-increasing distance between him and the world. But there is another possible answer, one which seems to transcend the boundaries of the novel. The castration symbolizes Lambert's true loss of humanity, literally the exhaustion of his manliness, his vitality. The final test put to him is a sentimental one. He fails due to an excess of love, and any kind of excess is fatal. Louis Lambert succeeds as an angel, but not as a man. Balzac's regard for the angelic state is well known, but his appraisal of basic human worth and the capacity for love is just as ap-parent. While no resolution is reached at the end of the novel, a dual impression is created. On the one hand, Louis Lambert and Pauline de Villenoix achieve a kind of perfect marriage, a spiritual bond that traverses this world and the next. Louis has sublimated his being, detached himself from his body, and become the essence of his existence. His vegetal silence, opposed to his unheard communion with the spheres, testifies to his success. But there is no way to efface the final, dreadful image of Lambert the man. "Alas! Already wrinkled, his hair white, the light was gone from his eyes which had become as vitreous as a blind man's. All his features seemed drawn toward the top of his head by a convulsion. . . . He seemed like remains torn from a tomb, a kind of victory of life over death, or death over life" (ibid., pp. 445–46). His treason to the human kind is made for a noble cause, but it is treason nonetheless. This walking cadaver somehow lessens the praise that the author appears to give to the philosopher. The eyes devoid of light, those eternal signs of men's intelligence and humanity, put a shadow over Lambert's achievement, and the angels do not seem quite as white. As for the marriage between Louis and Pauline, after the hero's death we learn that "Villenoix is falling into ruin" (ibid., p. 456).

The failure of the genius may be defined as an inability to communicate. Louis Lambert goes beyond the Word. Pauline describes his incoherence as a result of thinking principally done in a nonverbal medium. Ordinary mortals are permitted to hear only fragments of Lambert's celestial musings. The problem of Gambara the musician is very similar and gives us perhaps an even more revealing insight into one of Balzac's particular aesthetic dilemmas. For the author, the Word is at once the ship that goes on the delightful voyages so dear to Lambert and the cramped prison of purely verbal expression. Balzac rests uneasily with the need to express the inexpressible, his artistry seeking clarity of utterance, his poetic mysticism seeking a form that suggests transport. Music is seized upon as the ideal vehicle. "You only see what the painting shows you, you only hear what the poet tells you: music goes considerably beyond" (*Gambara, 9, 436*). Music, liberated from the precision of Word or Image, occupies a privileged place among the arts. It is a representation of the infinite.

> Are not Religion, Love and Music the triple expression of a single fact, the need for expansion which animates any noble soul? These three poetries go completely to God, who unravels all earthly emotions. This sainted

> human Trinity also participates in the infinite grandeur
> of God, whom we never imagine without surrounding
> Him with the fires of love, with the golden sistrums of
> music, light, and harmony. (*La Duchesse de Langeais*, 5,
> 133)

Music alone suggests to men a miraculous other world. "The
mind of the writer does not produce similar enjoyments, because what we paint is finite, determined, and what Beethoven
offers is infinite."[4]

As well as opening the gates of paradise, music unlocks the
door of the soul. Gambara says, "music alone has the power to
make us return to ourselves" (*Gambara*, 9, 436). It is the most
perfect representation of what is best in men. "To listen to
music is to love better the one you love" (ibid., p. 436).

One would expect the hero-musician to be one of the most
attractive characters in *La Comédie humaine*, embodying the
author's personal and literary aspirations. Yet Gambara meets
the fate reserved for all the true geniuses in Balzac's world, a
noble fate touched with a hint of degradation. Gambara translates the music of the spheres into a musical language decipher-
able only by its creator. The celestial harmonies conceived by
his mind's ear are unintelligible to other men. Beauty becomes
ugliness; order is rendered chaotic; and as Gambara plays the
score of his opera, *Mahomet*, the listeners are assailed with an
unbearable cacophony. The world rejects him with vehemence.
We are reminded of Louis Lambert's castigation at the hands of
Father Haugoult, as Gambara's music is sold at public auction.
"The day after the sale, these scores wrapped butter, fish and
fruit at the market" (ibid., p. 470). Balzac reserves particularly
inglorious ends for these sublime products of human genius.
He betrays their nature by imposing upon them the utility and
reality they seek to transcend. The final scenes of these two
novels spring from a common irony. The thinker steps outside

4. Balzac, *Lettres à l'Étrangère* (Paris, 1899), *1*, 398.

a mortal sphere and expresses his thought through a form of
madness, an inversion of philosophical clairvoyance. The exalted musician achieves his greatest success as a poor street-
singer. At the end of the novella we see Gambara and his wife
begging. "They both stood before the fashionable world which
was seated on chairs, and one of the greatest geniuses of this
time, the unknown Orpheus of modern music, played fragments of his scores. These pieces were so remarkable that they
wrenched a few pennies from Parisian indolence" (ibid., pp.
471–72). In this climactic moment, dramatically sharpened
by the author's feeling for contrast, Gambara's defeat is ambiguous, for it straddles the domains of humanity and art. It must
be examined in the light of the whole novella.

Gambara is noble but at the same time pathetically foolish.
He is also a cuckold, and beneath the fabric of his musical
flights, there lies the seduction of his wife Marianna by Count
Andrea Marcosini. Music is the pretext used by the Italian
nobleman to gain access to the beautiful Marianna. Balzac puts
Gambara in a most unflattering light, emphasizing his indiffer-
ence to his wife, the comic extent of his distraction. He uses the
same technique of characterization in the case of Balthazar
Claës, the hero of *La Recherche de l'absolu*. Here the scientist
is dumbly oblivious to the destruction of his family, the de-
crepitude of his house, the death of his wife, and his own
dehumanization. The failure of these geniuses is eventually
reduced to the most elemental of human referents—the surrender of their manhood. Louis Lambert attempts self-castration; Claës barters with his daughter the rights of paternity
in exchange for the money which will allow him to continue
his search for the absolute; Gambara plays his strange instrument, the panharmonicon, while his friend seduces his wife;
the tenor Genovese, of *Massimilla Doni*, becomes impotent
under the influence of his heavenly love for la Tinti. The roles
of lover, father, and husband are betrayed to the irresistible call
from the world beyond. Within the context of *La Comédie*

humaine these acts of treason cannot be tolerated, for they pervert the human vitality that pulsates through the universe and the order that shapes it.

Balzac's ambiguous attitude toward the genius is corroborated by the distorted works of art that are this figure's trademark. Gambara is at once less and more than an artist. The acuteness of his condition is made apparent by his inability to communicate in an art form in which intelligibility is not the goal. Beethoven harmonically transports the listener; Gambara dissonantly revolts him. Yet there are two moments when the musician transmits the beauty of his creation. These seem to be unusual examples of artistic cowardice on the part of Balzac. He is reluctant to admit that Gambara's message is uncommunicable, that the musician addresses himself to an audience of angels rather than men. Frenhofer, the painter-genius of *Le Chef-d'oeuvre inconnu,* is permitted no such moment of grace. His failure is resolved in self-doubt, madness, and suicide, while Gambara drifts along in the placid conviction that his is a valid aesthetics. Balzac's disapproval of this traitor to art is revealed in a letter to Madame Hanska.

> *Massimilla Doni* and *Gambara* represent, in the "Études philosophiques," the appearance of music under the double form of execution and composition; they are subjected to the same test as is thought in *Louis Lambert,* that is to say the work and its execution killed by a too great abundance of the creative principle, which *Le Chef-d'oeuvre inconnu* dictated to me for painting.[5]

The most eloquent failure of Gambara is, however, the one he passes on to Balzac. Like Lambert, the musician upsets the author's relationship with the Word, forcing him to abandon its poetic thoroughly artistic qualities in favor of flat, rational expression. Gambara's wrongheaded appraisal of his form's

5. Ibid., pp. 398–99.

potential corresponds to Balzac's belief that music can be translated by the most unmusical elements within the Word. The
scores of Meyerbeer's *Robert le Diable* and Gambara's *Mahomet* receive endless pages of pseudo-technical description,
with great flourishes of keys, choruses, and chords. The same
process is repeated in *Massimilla Doni,* where Rossini's *Mosè*
earns for itself the dubious honor of Balzac's musicological
analysis. He borrows the technique from the music critic, and
it is one that disturbs the fictional texture of his novels. The
Word, used imaginatively to describe the world, becomes
reticent before art.

Balzac reveals the most original aspect of his literary nature when he searches for the music native to the Word. In
Z. Marcas, he writes a poem about the failure of a genius, which
takes its rhythm from the Word.

Z. Marcas is a genius in the field of politics, incongruent
because of his honesty and therefore doomed to failure. The
story of his life is sketchily recounted. It is merely a peg upon
which the author attaches a sonic and visual representation of
failure. His intention is revealed in the first paragraph. "There
was a certain harmony between the person and the name. This
Z which preceded Marcas, seen on the address of his letters,
and which he never forgot in his signature, this last letter of the
alphabet, suggested to the mind something fatal" (*Z. Marcas,*
7, 736). The reader receives this knowledge as a warning of the
irrevocability of Marcas' destiny, of its sadness and tragic end.
The story is to be read with this constantly in mind. Each of
the protagonist's remarks, each of his actions, the events of his
past and present, all are to be weighed and measured against
this gloomy introduction. Here again we see the author bolster-
ing the reader's credence by placing him in a position of
omniscience.

Balzac attaches special importance to the name of his hero because he truly believes that names do have meaning. If a man's

face is capable of revealing his destiny, why not his name? Balzac forces attention upon the aural and visual aspects of the Word. In it one can perceive the summary of a man's life. "MARCAS! Repeat this two-syllabled name to yourself; do you not find it has a sinister meaning? Does it not seem to you that the man who carries it will be martyred?" (ibid., p. 736) The reader, with senses perhaps less acute than those of the author, might fail to see, without his aid, the great meaning stored in the name. Balzac first tries to convince with the enthusiasm of his rhetoric. Then he constructs a veritable monument revealing all the qualities of the name. We learn that it is the name of a man to be reckoned with, an important man, hence one who should command our attention and evoke our sympathy with his fall.

> Although strange and savage, this name is nevertheless worthy of posterity; it is well composed, it is easily pronounced, it has that brevity necessary to famous names. Is it not as sweet as it is bizarre? But does it not also seem unfinished? I would not like to take it upon myself to affirm that names exert no influence over destiny. Between the facts of life and the names of men, there are secret and inexplicable concordances or visible discordances which surprise; often distant, but efficacious correlations are revealed there. Our globe is full, everything holds together in it. Perhaps some day we will return to the Occult Sciences. (ibid., p. 736)

In a reference to the metaphysical density of the world, where everything has a reason, where the slightest detail impinges on the totality of life and of course upon each man's destiny, Balzac integrates the name of Z. Marcas with the masterplan of *La Comédie humaine*. The creator of a universe so tied up with inner rhythms and resounding with so many echoes does not hesitate to imply that the germs of a character's failure can be found in the physical qualities of his name.

> Examine again this name: Z. Marcas! The man's whole
> life is in the fantastic assemblage of these seven letters.
> Seven, the most significant of the cabalistic numbers. Man
> dies at thirty-five, thus his life is composed of seven lus-
> trums. Marcas! Don't you have the impression of some-
> thing precious which is broken in a fall, with or without
> noise? (ibid., p. 737)

The name, used as a vocative, resounds grandly in this passage.
Balzac assails us with references to it, fabrications upon it, evidence of its special qualities. Numbers, kabala, and death impart additional stature to the hero, who, by the way, has not
yet been introduced. And then, whether we believe it or not,
we are prepared to accept Balzac's fiction about the name. He
lures the mind with the magic of the Word, repeating it like
an incantation. Perhaps it does suggest something precious that
breaks in a fall. Such an interpretation is at least possible.

The author has by no means exhausted the qualities of the
Word. He sees in the construction of the letter Z "a frustrated
twist," "a tormented life" (ibid., pp. 736–37), both signs of
deviation. With the addition of the kabala and number symbolism the author succeeds in cutting this character loose from
reality, depicting his oddness, making him seem a creature ill-
adapted to a material existence. This impression is entirely
correct. The undoing of Marcas is the fact that he is out of
tune with the demands of reality; he is another of Balzac's
incongruents.

Throughout the story Marcas' failure is seen in his head,
his face, his eyes, and through the imagination of his young
friends. They call him "the ruins of Palmyra" (ibid., p. 742),
sharing the author's joy in poeticizing failure, attracted for
artistic reasons to the pile of debris that is Z. Marcas. Yet they
too are eventually taken in by the Word. It becomes for them
a poem of defeat.

We then learned that magic name of Z. Marcas. Like the
children we were, we repeated more than a hundred times,
with the most varied intonations, absurd and melancholy,
that name whose pronunciation lent itself to our game.
Justin succeeded occasionally in emitting the Z like a
firecracker at its departure, and, after having brilliantly
deployed the name's first syllable, he depicted a fall in the
abrupt hollowness with which he pronounced the last.
(ibid., pp. 742–43)

One feels irresistibly drawn into the childish game, and the
letter Z comes to symbolize all that is strange and final. The
most striking image, however, is that of the firecracker, an
object that never really belongs to the earth until it dies, after
a long, quick fall. Z. Marcas is that firecracker, in his brilliance
and in his defeat, and Balzac's verbal music faithfully portrays
it.

CHAPTER 6

The Inevitable Verdict

It has become increasingly evident that one can validly discuss
the typical character in *La Comédie humaine*. If a lesson is to
be learned from the categorization of failure, it is that the
divisions are most emphatically arbitrary. They are useful only
in clarification, in an effort to impose some kind of form onto
the sprawling matter under analysis. The vocabulary used to
describe the different examples bears, through necessity, a
sameness, a ring of familiarity. The rhetorical devices used in
the case of Lucien de Rubempré can be discerned in the presen-
tations of César Birotteau and Louis Lambert. Balzac fervently
believes that "there is only one animal" (Avant-propos à *La
Comédie humaine*). Man is a single animal type. All men are
subject to the same pressures, the same laws. The failures that
result from weakness are also infected by a certain amount of
blindness. The genius type might just as accurately be characterized as blind and passionate. Finally, all the failures in *La
Comédie humaine* should be ascribed to the single fault of
incongruence.

This incongruence is most poignantly and concisely drama-
tized in the case of Colonel Chabert, the one figure in *La
Comédie humaine* who is physically and officially divorced from
reality. The very embodiment of incongruence, he is completely

cut off from time. He lives without name, without identity. As far as the world is concerned, he is a dead man and therefore can exert no will. The fact that Colonel Chabert is alive, though in some ways dead, is manifested in his physical being and in his clothing, symbolic extensions of his inner being and unmistakable signals for the reader. "His neck was tightly encircled by a miserable tie of black silk" (*Le Colonel Chabert*, 2, 1096). The black necktie seems to be part of the ideal frame for this portrait of death. The brim of Chabert's hat complements this effect. "The brim of the hat which covered the old man's forehead projected a black furrow upon the upper part of his face. Through the bluntness of the contrast, this bizarre, although natural effect put into relief the white wrinkles, the cold sinuosities, the discolored sentiment of this cadaverous face" (ibid., p. 1096). Death is written on this man's face. He has no business among the living, and the remainder of his fictional life is grim proof of his incongruence. Balzac is careful in this first, long description of the hero to emphasize his death-like characteristics. "Finally, the absence of any movement in the body, of any warmth in the glance, harmonized with a certain expression of dolorous madness, with the degrading symptoms by which idiocy is characterized, to make of this face something deadly, that no human word could express" (ibid., p. 1096). Colonel Chabert is not mad. His expression is simply that of a man who no longer sees as other men do. He has known death and now lives with its imprint on his face. Without a name, deprived of his official existence, which truly defined his relation to other men, he cannot survive.

Chabert's great mistake is that he attempts to return to the living. Taken for dead at the battle of Eylau, a victim of amnesia, he has ceased to exist in the eyes of the law. His wife has inherited his fortune and remarried. He attempts to reclaim his name and, in doing so, dies a second death infinitely more horrible than the first. At least at Eylau he died a hero. Before learning the final truth about his wife's baseness, he asks her: "Are the dead then wrong in coming back?" (ibid., p. 1135). He should have known the answer. Chabert submits to many deceptions before realizing that his position is a false and impossible one. Thoroughly disgusted by the extent to which self-interest degrades humanity, a process he has witnessed most brutally in the actions of his own wife, he disowns his name and, in fact, abdicates his status in society. He therefore admits to his own incongruence. "You cannot know the extent of my disdain for this exterior life which the majority of men prize. I have suddenly been seized by a disease: disgust for humanity" (ibid., p. 1144). Chabert has seen humanity with the kind of detachment that only a "live" dead man can enjoy, and he has learned a bitter lesson. What is incongruent to reality has lost its right to existence.

Years later, the lawyer Derville, a witness to the tragedy of Colonel Chabert, sees this wreck of a human being at the side of a road. Derville says to a friend: "That old man . . . is a poem, or as the romantics say, a drama" (ibid., p. 1145). Truly the story of Colonel Chabert is a poem, a dramatization of failure. Balzac has created a situation in which a human being judges life from the vantage point of death. He has created a character who perfectly symbolizes his theory that fitting into reality, functioning within the framework of a given society, and reacting to its ever-changing demands are prime requisites for success, life, mere survival.

The author's values give impulse and conviction to the omnipresent rule of congruence. These values, introduced in the first chapter, are political, moral, and literary. In fact, they belong to all these categories at once. The conservatism that colors Balzac's views on government and religion reflects his desire (a noticeably frustrated one) to tie together in some way the numerous and opposing aspects of life. For fleeting moments the author deludes himself into believing that an order can be imposed upon the hydra of existence. This tendency on his part is seen in the Dantesque arrangement that *La Comédie humaine* was supposed to have taken in its final version. Although Balzac fulfills his literary plan to a great extent, the penetrating artist's eye lodged within him perceives the impracticability of his social, political, and religious ideas. This same eye does not, however, lose its avidity for order, its need to find a pattern in disorder. The artistic solution lies in the Word, while the human one is defined by the now-familiar construct wherein men must obey the most immediate demands of the moment. They must, in other words, conform to the virtually unpredictable currents of reality. The character who turns his back to the whirlpool, voluntarily or not, faces instead his own failure.

Failure not only lurks menacingly in the world imagined by the author; it shares in the fabrication of his novels. We have already suggested that the rule of congruence and its close relative, failure, weigh heavily upon the lives of each of the characters. These two references are provided to bolster the reader's credence. A life can be judged and measured in relation to such constants. The author very cleverly exploits the device of an unchanging background, which is like the shadow cast by the fiction's thickness, a thickness compounded by the expected and the eternal. Belief in a character who functions within such a large context is subtly elicited. He takes on an existence that goes beyond the dimensions of a single novel, even beyond the body of *La Comédie humaine*. He enters that region of immutable laws and forces that is reality, the reality that everyone perceives at its most elementary level. It is an essentially lawless system, and if the good die young, their death has nothing to do with their goodness. Balzac is exploiting here a fundamental of human nature, the conviction that nothing succeeds like the ability and will to succeed. Therefore, when the reader sees that the fictional character is a victim of stupidity, blindness, or any number of obvious defects, he can be sure that this character is on the road to failure. This is the way it usually happens in real life; this is the way it happens in *La Comédie humaine.*

Having thus engaged his audience, Balzac has won a great battle. The credibility granted to the characters is naturally transferred in some measure to the plot. In fact, the peripeties of plot remain somehow extraneous to the truth of Balzac's novels. Surprising occurrences that dot a man's destiny tend to lose their importance if the totality of this destiny is convincing. By believing in the character, one is strongly tempted to believe in the events that comprise his life. Thus, the thickening process, the urge to give weight to stuff wrought by a facile imagination, is served. Failure gives a shape to this thickness and a direction to this weight. Each character carries within himself the germ of failure. The working out of his destiny is an attempt to prevent its flowering in brazen defiance of a world designed to nurture this germ by putting the human being into countless menacing situations.

As we have seen, Balzac's views on failure fit extremely well into his aesthetics. But even when divorced from the context of the author's convictions, failure displays great, if more traditional, literary utility. For instance, an obviously revealing relationship can be obtained from the opposition of failure and success. Balzac's fondness for such contrasts is by now familiar. We have seen him juxtapose a character's future failure upon his present success, as in the first pages of *César Birotteau.* The successful dandy, de Marsay, is the brilliant image of success in which Lucien de Rubempré sees reflected his own image of shabby failure. The luster of Valérie Marneffe's salon is intensified when seen next to the miserable apartment of Adeline Hulot.

Furthermore, the progression of the novel is dependent upon the developments in the protagonist's life, which are described as functions of failure and success. So often in *La Comédie humaine* we see the hero hurtling downward, finding himself face to face with failure at the end of the novel. This rhythm, governed by the false steps taken by the central character, can be seen vividly in the final pages of each section in *Illusions perdues* and in the conclusions of novels like *Le Cabinet des antiques, Une Fille d'Eve, Le Curé de Tours,* and *Le Colonel Chabert.* In fact, it is difficult to find a Balzac novel where this descent toward failure does not appear.

This failure has a wide spectrum of tonality. The comic failure of the Chevalier de Valois in *La Vieille fille* is counterpointed by the poignant one of Athanase Granson in the same novel. The totally unsympathetic character of Victurnien d'Esgrignon merits a detailed, clinical account of failure, providing a pivot for the essentially political novel, *Le Cabinet des antiques.* The most resounding human failures, however, are those of characters like Goriot, Hulot, and César Birotteau. The author's attitude toward these creations is, as we have demonstrated, ambivalent, confused by a mixture of disgust and compassion. But if one seeks the figure of the tragic hero in *La Comédie humaine* these are the most likely candidates. Their ruin is so complete, their destruction so gruesome, the author's tone so grandly black. The kind of physical and moral agony that accompanies the last hours of Goriot rivals the wails and shrieks attendant upon the catastrophe of the classical Greek tragedy. Yet the analogy is not a fruitful one, for it does an injustice to the uniqueness of both forms. The flaw of Goriot is not hubris; it is not even a flaw. Goriot is consumed by a malignant disease, which imposes itself upon his whole being. His fatherly passion does not exist in a broad structure of personality, nor does it take relief from an obviously noble stature. The bolsters of gods, myth, and tradition are denied Balzac. Since the exterior frame of reference for this hero is so limited, his scope springs from an inner source. The whole notion of a fall from a noble estate must be translated into new terms. Society is riddled with varying degrees of degradation and excludes absolute standards against which human worth is judged. The feeling generated by a Balzacian failure does not

come from a perception of the distance between a superior
order and the individual, because the functioning order is not
superior; it simply is. The fact that Goriot is out of tune with
things is not intrinsically tragic, because the things with which
he is out of tune have no transcendental value.

This is the point at which most of Balzac's theoretical pronouncements must be discarded, and the outline of his particular
page allowed to dominate. This is where categorization and
synthesis lead us away from the truth. In the context of what is
tragic in Balzac, his statement that "there is only one animal"
has no relevance. It is only a tool that puts in order the motors
of our realization, making us aware of failure's occurrence and
convincing us of its truth. Then, the process of particularization
takes over. Goriot ceases to be the generalized, mythified Christ
of Paternity and becomes a tangible construct, with features we
touch, with a voice we hear, with differentiated accessories that
define the separate moments of his existence. These moments
are precious because they are touched, seen, and heard. Intimacy
and familiarity are the measure of their worth, and in the
fullness of their enumeration they become ours. In this way,
Balzac's rhetoric imposes stature upon the meanest of lives,
and significantly, it is a stature that needs no context other
than the fiction that gives it birth. Goriot literally falls from
himself. The Word is the locus, pinpointing him, bringing
him into close perspective, and transforming his destruction
into the destruction of the known. Balzac plays upon the
reader's sense of possession and turns Goriot's death into a
personal loss. Like Rastignac, we are given access to the facts
and things of a life, and this participation gives us the right
to share the young man's grief. It is a grief that survives sober
objectivity, because it wells from a perception of the only
truth: Goriot lived; he was human. The comfortable distance
that separates art and the spectator in the classical tradition is
obliterated. The different exigencies of theater and novel account for some of this, but the basic distinguishing factor is

qualitative. Tragedy is designed to resolve itself in a catharsis of pity and fear, sounding in its wake the eternal human experience. A sense of the eternal is present in *La Comédie humaine,* but any comfort it offers is nullified by the suffocating immediacy achieved as the fiction is thrust, in all its unavoidable detail, upon the squirming and grieving reader. The tragic experience must be redefined in this way in order to have a place in *La Comédie humaine.*

For Balzac, failure leaves an uneradicable imprint upon human existence. He judges life by its standard; he nurtures art with its inspiration. Very conveniently, the reader is provided with an image of the author in the body of *La Comédie humaine.* Refracted through the character of Gobseck we can perceive Balzac's relationship to his fictional universe and the role that failure plays therein.

Gobseck the moneylender dominates the lives of his debtors in the same way that the author controls the destinies of his fictional children. Since gold is the true base of society, since only money is viable in Balzac's world, the source of money is the source of power; it is creativity. Gobseck's command of the world through money is so complete that it renders him omniscient. In fact, due to his special qualities, no power can challenge him. "My glance is like that of God, I see into hearts. Nothing is hidden from me. You refuse nothing to the man who ties and unties the purse-strings" (*Gobseck, 2, 636*). Life passes before the eyes of Gobseck in all its nakedness, without shame, declaiming its needs with the honesty of despair. No one but the author has this god-like vantage point. Both Gobseck and Balzac have the power of life and death over their subjects.

Gobseck has the privilege of reading into the souls of the desperate people forced to come to him. He examines men who are on the verge of failure, their nerves quivering under his clear scrutiny. "No one having any credit at the Bank comes into my shop, where the first step made from my door to my office proclaims despair, a failure ready to burst forth, and in particular a refusal of money by all the bankers. I only see stags at bay, tracked by their pack of creditors" (ibid., pp. 630–31). It is in this atmosphere of crisis that failure takes on its full significance. Failure is the sum of a life. At the moment of ruin one removes the disguise, however imperfectly it has been worn, and the whole truth is revealed. Witnessing this process is an important and moving experience. Gobseck is aware of this and appreciates his position.

> Do you believe that it is a small matter to penetrate thus the most secret recesses of the human heart, to take up the life of others, to see it naked? The spectacles are always varied: hideous wounds, mortal sorrows, love scenes, miseries for which the waters of the Seine lie in wait, a young man's joys which lead to the scaffold, laughs of despair and sumptuous parties. Yesterday, a tragedy: some good-natured father asphyxiates himself because he can no longer feed his children. Tomorrow a comedy: a young man will try to play the scene of Monsieur Dimanche[1] for me, with the variations of our time. (ibid., p. 635)

In this passage Balzac extracts art from failure. He idealizes the privilege of Gobseck and, in doing so, explains his own attraction to ruin. The author exultantly embraces his creation in the most crucial moment of its existence, simply because it is then so true, so real, so vibrant. It is the finale of a human comedy where all is exposed in blazing clarity, where life exhibits itself in its most extreme aspects. Balzac, an artist of despair, sees a diseased life in a hideous wound, and the drama that precedes suicide is reflected in the waters of the Seine. He hears laughter in the voice of a doomed man and then creates a life to go with that laughter.

1. Molière, *Dom Juan*, IV.3.

Failure is a manifestation of the author's pessimism. In its more gruesome aspects, it is an outlet for his morbidity. Finally, it is one of the frontiers of *La Comédie humaine,* the point to which the characters inexorably march, amassing their lives on their shoulders as they go. At this frontier sits a judge with burning eyes, a man who, from this vantage point, chooses those who are fated to cross the border into the land of defeat.

Selected Bibliography

ABRAHAM, PIERRE, *Créatures chez Balzac*, Paris, Gallimard, 1931.

ALAIN, *Avec Balzac*, Paris, Gallimard, 1937.

ATKINSON, GEOFFROY, *Les Idées de Balzac d'après "La Comédie humaine,"* Geneva, Droz, 1949.

BALZAC, HONORÉ DE, *La Comédie humaine*, Paris, Bibliothèque de la Pléiade, 1935–62.

————, *Correspondance,* Textes réunis, classés et annotés par Roger Pierrot, 2 vols. Paris, Garnier, 1960–62.

————, *Illusions perdues,* Édition présentée par Gaëton Picon, Paris, Le Club du meilleur livre, 1958.

————, *Lettres à l'Étrangère,* ed. Louvenjoul et Bouteron, Paris, C. Lévy, 1899–1950.

————, *Oeuvres complètes,* Édition de M. Bouteron et H. Longnon, Paris, L. Conrad, 1912–40.

————, *Oeuvres complètes,* Édition de la Société des Études Balzaciennes, Paris, Le Prat, 1955–63.

————, *Pensées, sujets, fragmens,* Préface et notes de Jacques Crépet, Paris, Blaizot, 1910.

BARDÈCHE, MAURICE, *Balzac romancier,* Paris, Plon, 1940.

BEEBE, MAURICE, *Ivory Towers and Sacred Founts, the Artist as Hero in Fiction from Goethe to Joyce,* New York, New York University Press, 1964.

————, "The Lesson of Balzac's Artists," *Criticism,* 2 (1960), 221–41.

BÉGUIN, ALBERT, *Balzac visionnaire,* Geneva, Skira, 1946.

BELLESORT, ANDRÉ, *Balzac et son oeuvre,* Paris, Perrin & Cie, 1946.

BILLY, ANDRÉ, *Vie de Balzac,* Paris, Flammarion, 1944.

BOREL, JACQUES, *Personnages et destins balzaciens, la création littéraire et ses sources anecdotiques,* Paris, J. Corti, 1958.

CURTIUS, ERNST R., *Balzac,* Traduit de l'allemand par Henri Jourdan, Paris, B. Grasset, 1933.

EIGELDINGER, MARC, *La Philosophie de l'art chez Balzac,* Geneva, P. Cailler, 1957.

EMERY, LEON, *Balzac, les grands thèmes de "La Comédie humaine,"* Paris, Éditions Balzac, 1943.

FERNANDEZ, RAMON, *Balzac,* Paris, 1943.

FOREST, H., *L'Esthétique du roman balzacien,* Paris, Presses Universitaires de France, 1950.

GIRAUD, RAYMOND, *The Unheroic Hero in the Novels of Stendhal, Balzac and Flaubert,* New Brunswick, Rutgers University Press, 1957.

GUYON, BERNARD, *La Pensée politique et sociale de Balzac,* Paris, A. Colin, 1947.

LAUBRIET, P., *L'Intelligence de l'art chez Balzac: d'une esthétique balzacienne,* Paris, Didier, 1961.

LEVIN, HARRY, *The Gates of Horn,* New York, Oxford University Press, 1963.

MARCEAU, FÉLICIEN, *Balzac et son monde,* Paris, Gallimard, 1955.

OLIVER, E. J., *Balzac the European,* London, Sheed & Ward, 1959.

PICON, GAËTON, *Balzac par lui-même,* Paris, Éditions du Seuil, 1957.

POULET, GEORGES, "La Distance intérieure," *Études sur le temps humain* (2 vols. Paris, Plon, 1952), 2.

Index

(Works by Balzac are listed alphabetically under Balzac.)